Adult Color By Number Coloring Book

This Color by Number Book belongs to:

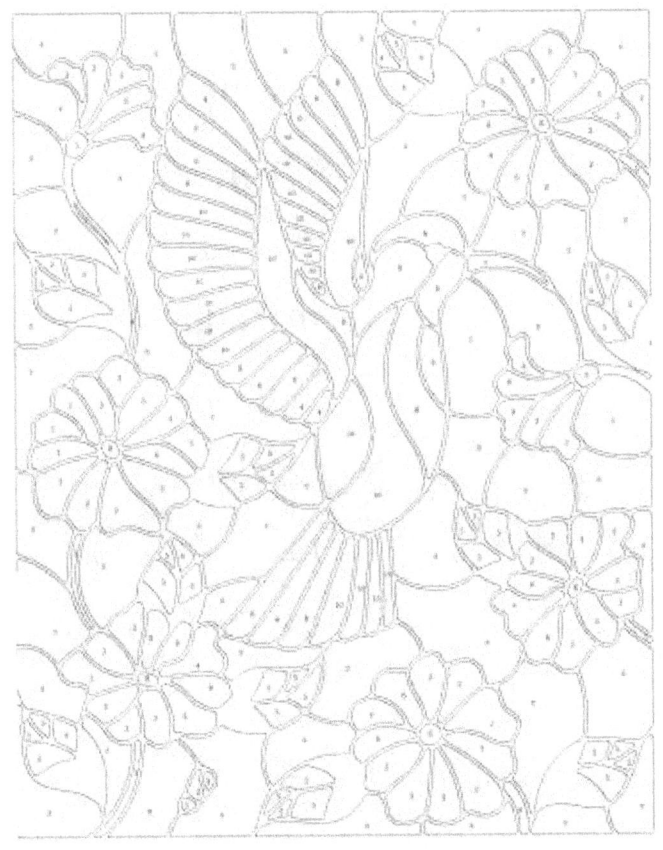

Copyright © 2020 Adult Puzzle Books

1. Black
2. Blue
3. Light Blue
4. Brown
5. Dark Red
6. Orange
7. Yellow
8. Purple
9. Pink
10. Gold
11. Green
12. Gold
13. Red
14. Dark Green

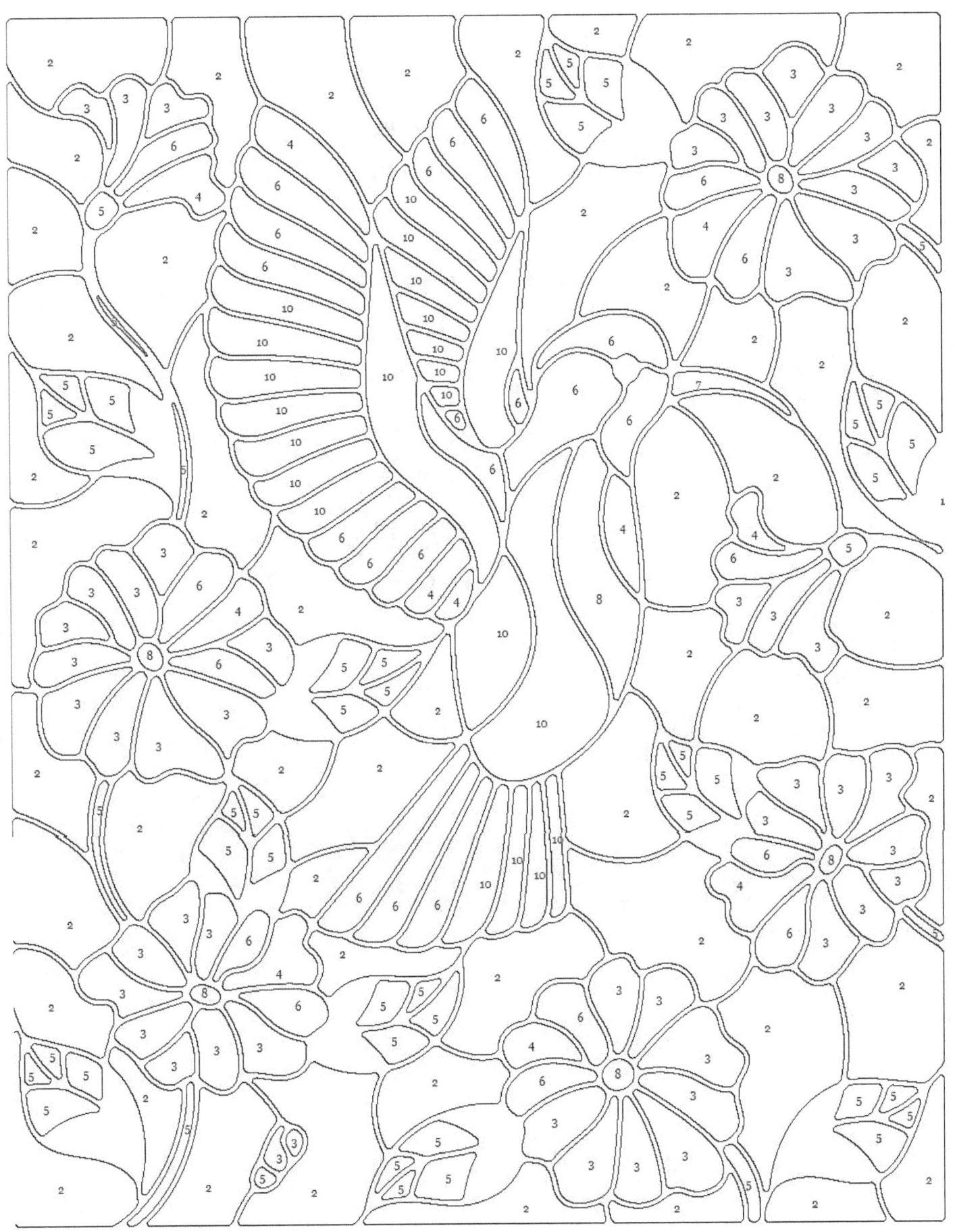

1. Black
2. Blue
3. Light Blue
4. Brown
5. Dark Red
6. Orange
7. Yellow
8. Purple
9. Pink
10. Gold
11. Green
12. Gold
13. Red
14. Dark Green

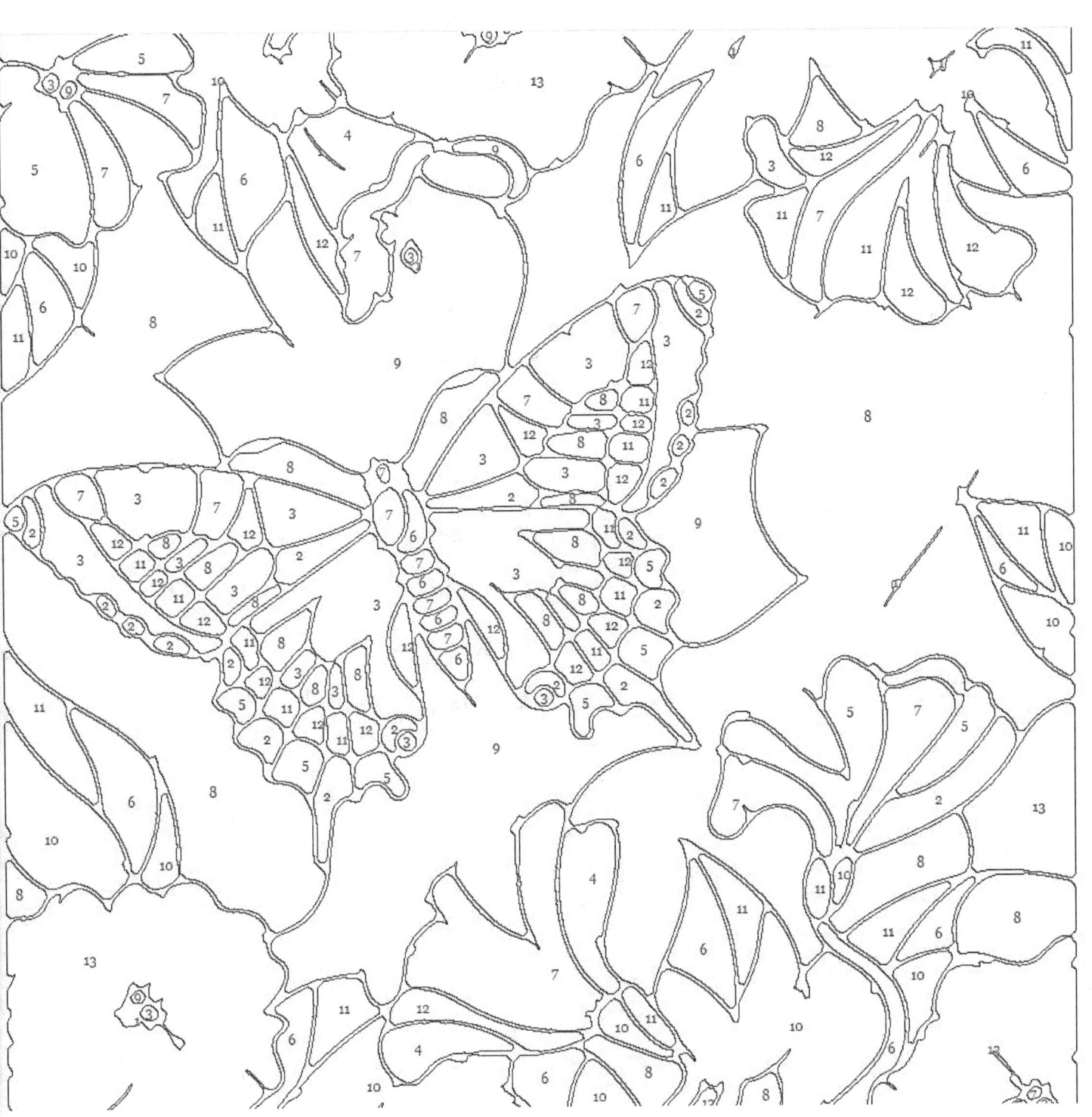

1. Black
2. Blue
3. Light Blue
4. Brown
5. Dark Red
6. Orange
7. Yellow
8. Purple
9. Pink
10. Gold
11. Green
12. Gold
13. Red
14. Dark Green

1. Black
2. Blue
3. Light Blue
4. Brown
5. Dark Red
6. Orange
7. Yellow
8. Purple
9. Pink
10. Gold
11. Green
12. Gold
13. Red
14. Dark Green

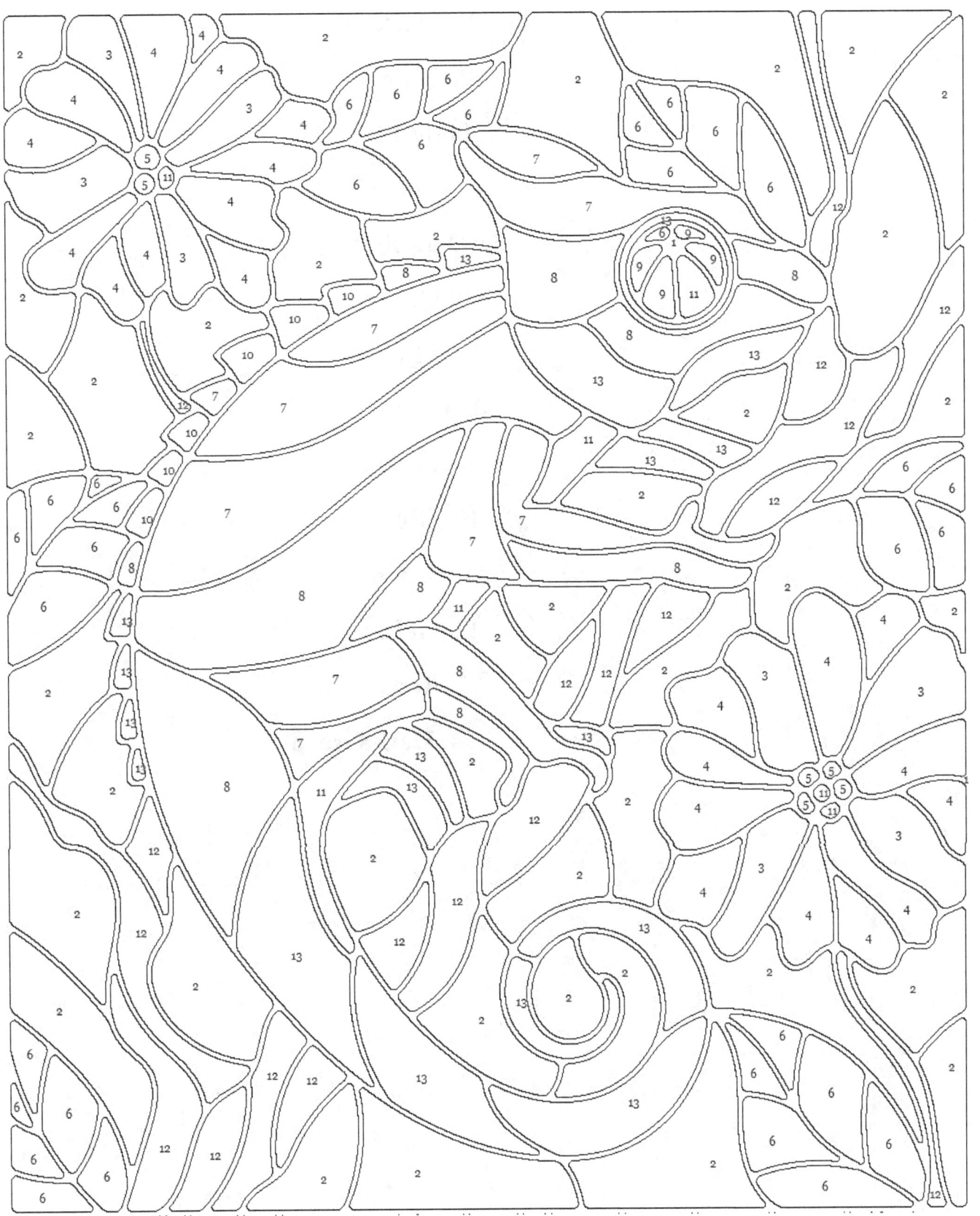

1. Black
2. Blue
3. Light Blue
4. Brown
5. Dark Red
6. Orange
7. Yellow
8. Purple
9. Pink
10. Gold
11. Green
12. Gold
13. Red
14. Dark Green

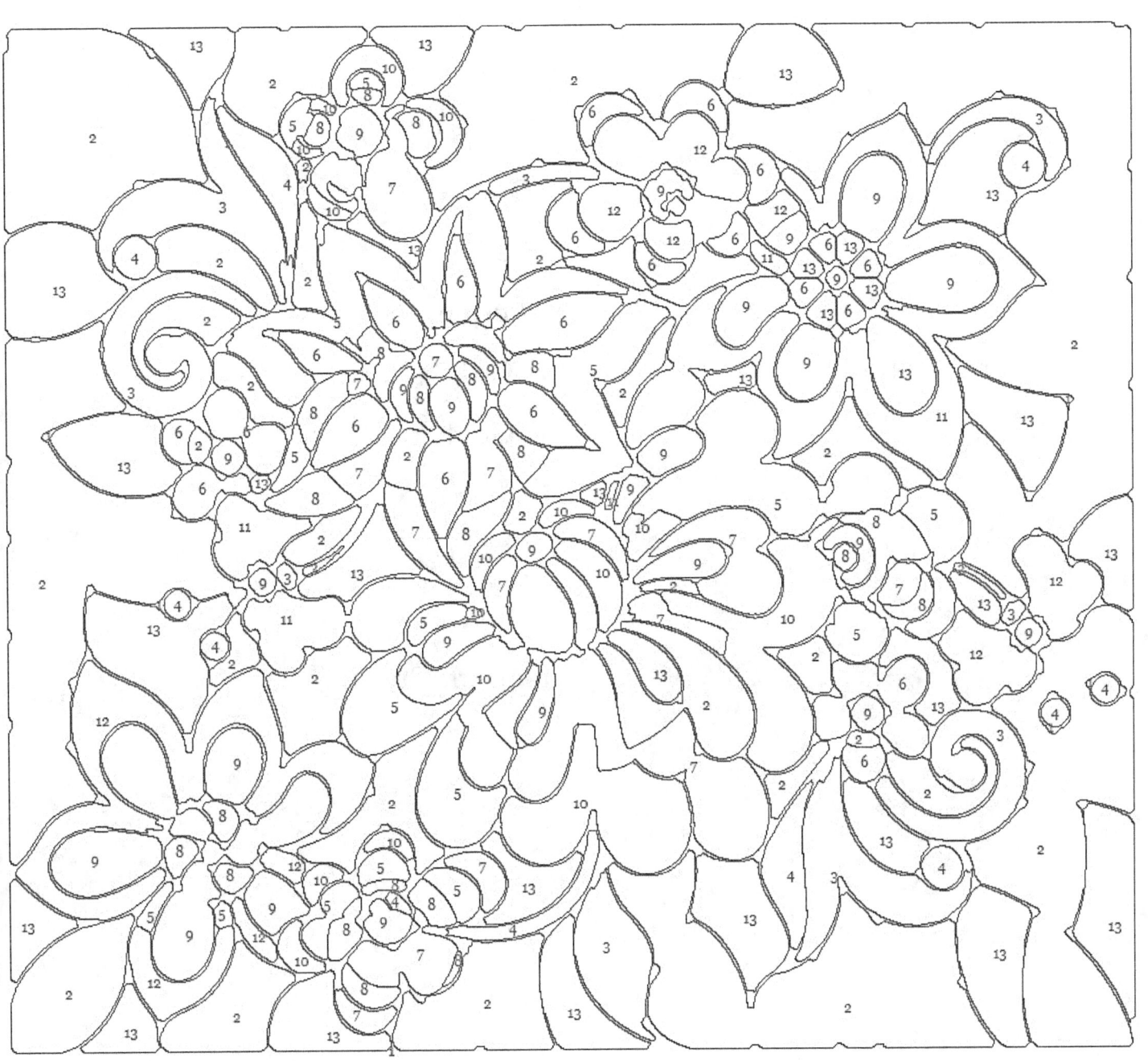

1. Black
2. Blue
3. Light Blue
4. Brown
5. Dark Red
6. Orange
7. Yellow
8. Purple
9. Pink
10. Gold
11. Green
12. Gold
13. Red
14. Dark Green

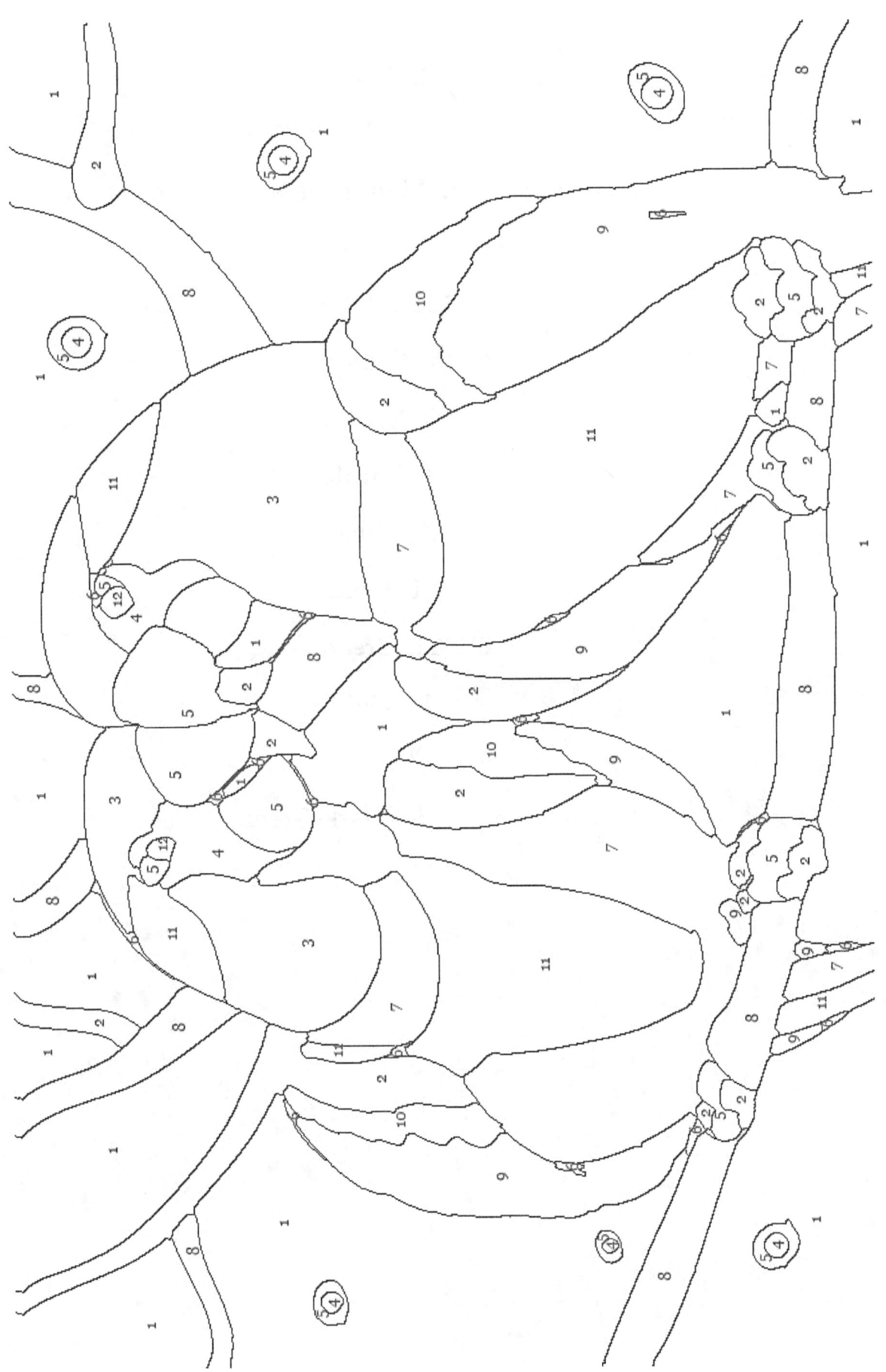

1. Black
2. Blue
3. Light Blue
4. Brown
5. Dark Red
6. Orange
7. Yellow
8. Purple
9. Pink
10. Gold
11. Green
12. Gold
13. Red
14. Dark Green

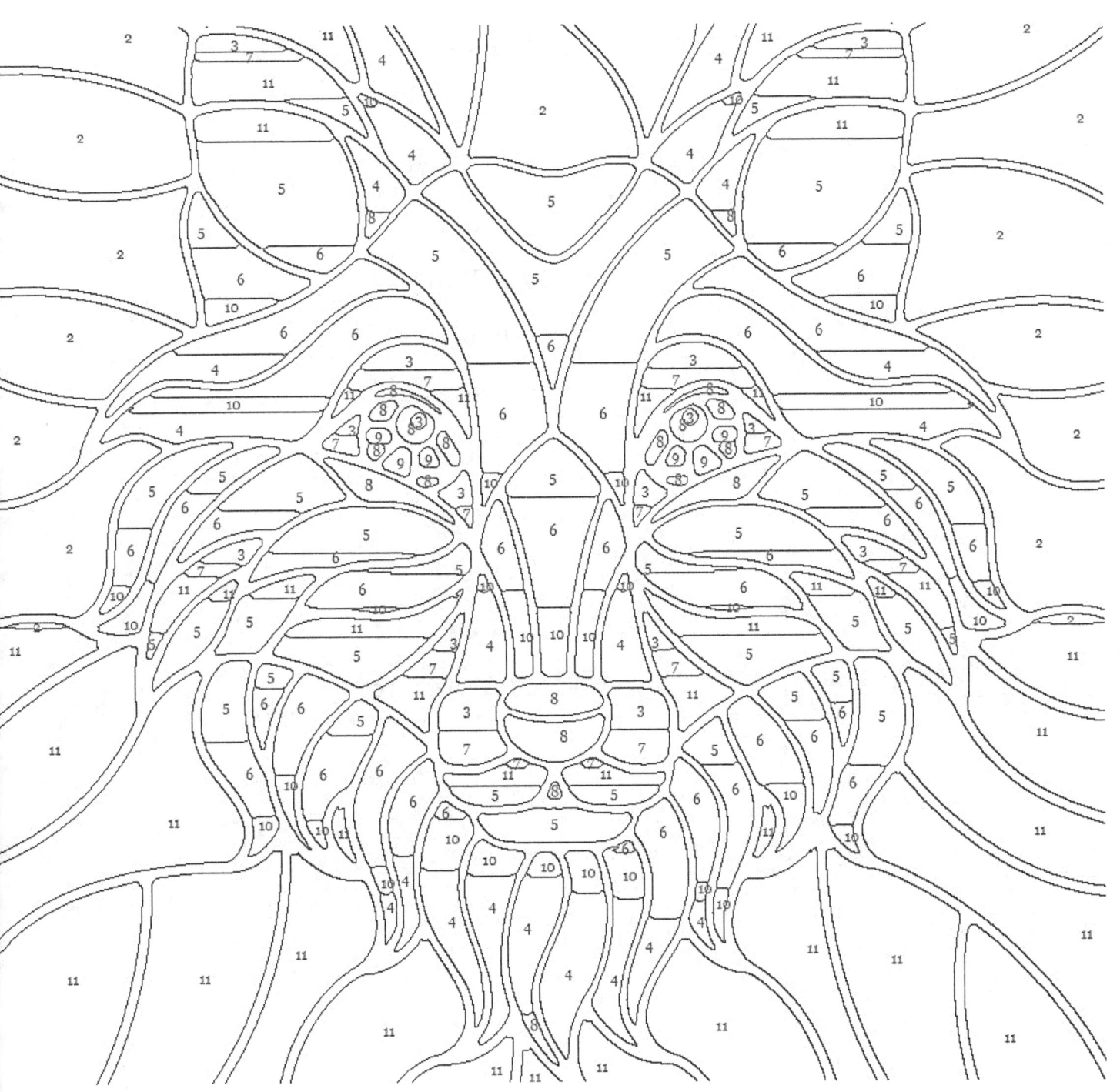

1. Black
2. Blue
3. Light Blue
4. Brown
5. Dark Red
6. Orange
7. Yellow
8. Purple
9. Pink
10. Gold
11. Green
12. Gold
13. Red
14. Dark Green

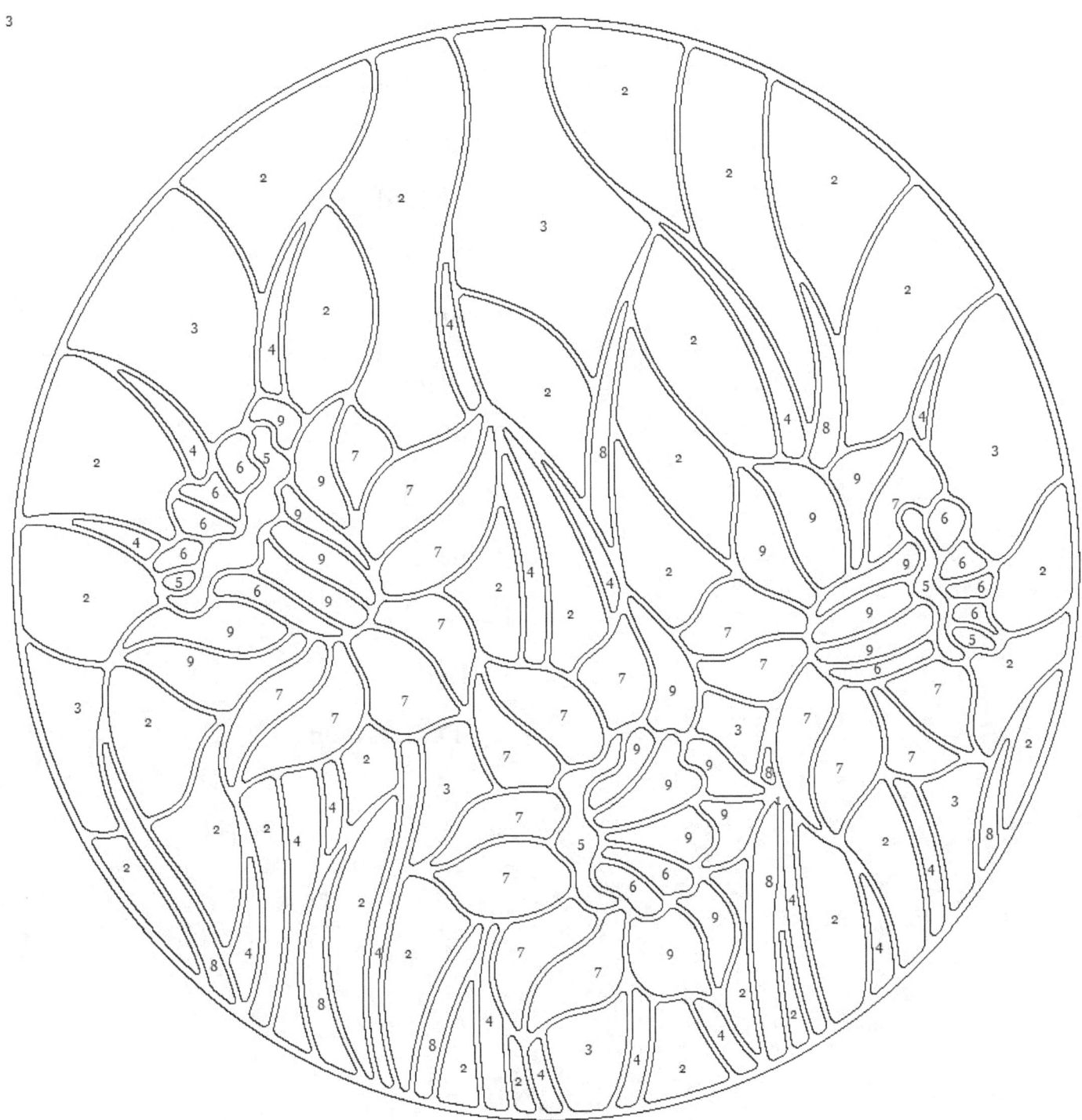

1. Black
2. Blue
3. Light Blue
4. Brown
5. Dark Red
6. Orange
7. Yellow
8. Purple
9. Pink
10. Gold
11. Green
12. Gold
13. Red
14. Dark Green

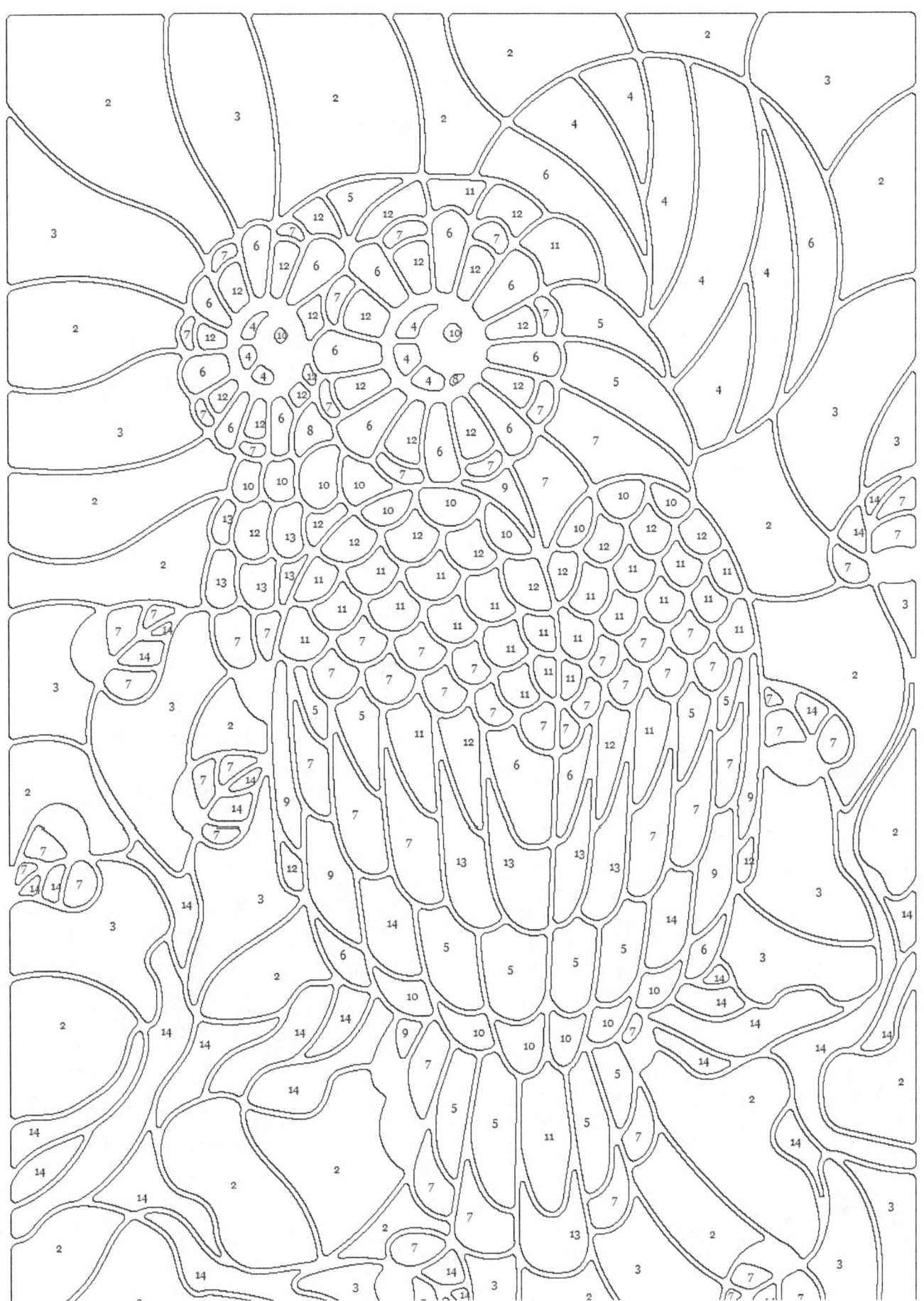

1. Black
2. Blue
3. Light Blue
4. Brown
5. Dark Red
6. Orange
7. Yellow
8. Purple
9. Pink
10. Gold
11. Green
12. Gold
13. Red
14. Dark Green

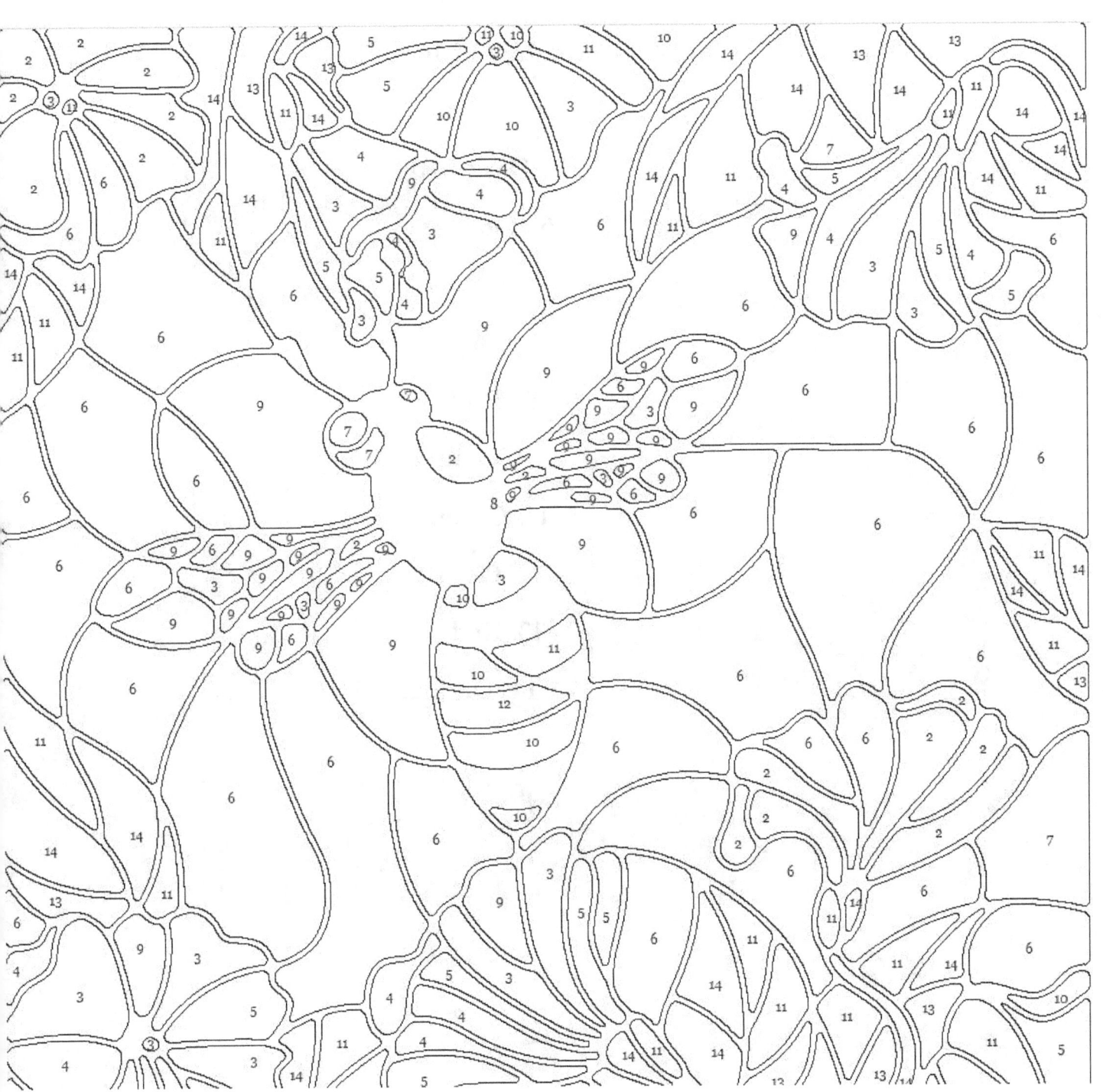

1. Black
2. Blue
3. Light Blue
4. Brown
5. Dark Red
6. Orange
7. Yellow
8. Purple
9. Pink
10. Gold
11. Green
12. Gold
13. Red
14. Dark Green

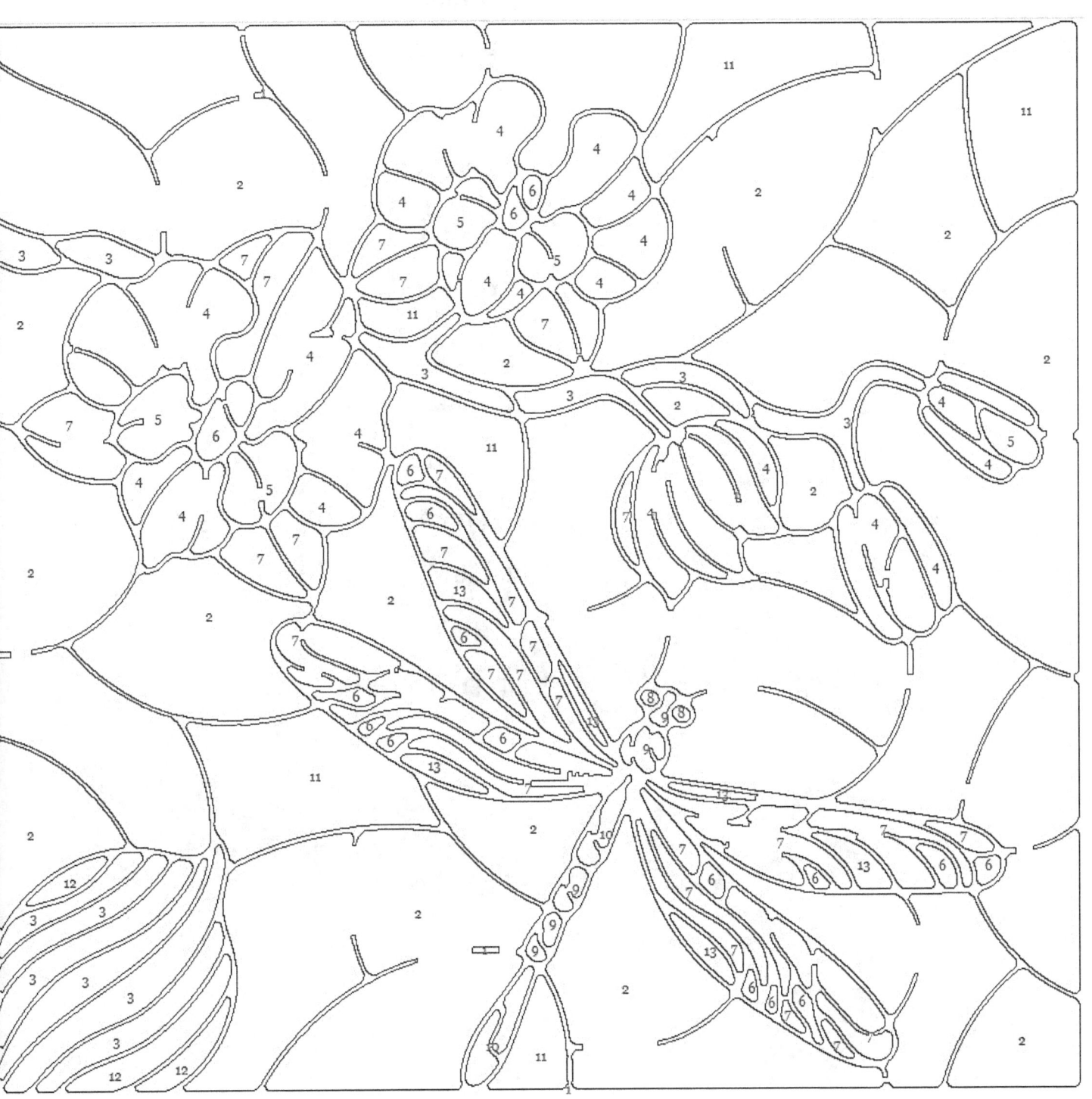

1. Black
2. Blue
3. Light Blue
4. Brown
5. Dark Red
6. Orange
7. Yellow
8. Purple
9. Pink
10. Gold
11. Green
12. Gold
13. Red
14. Dark Green

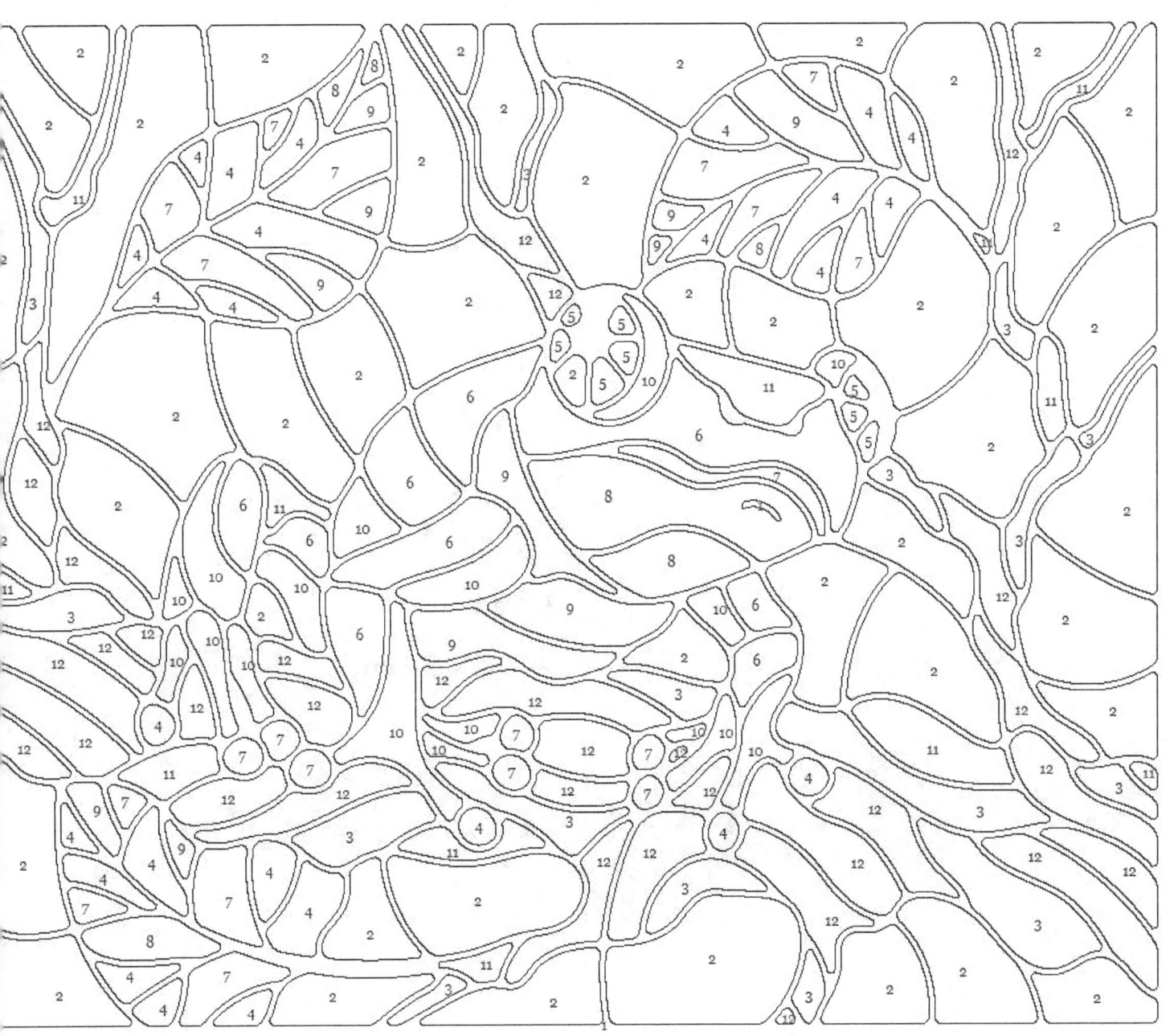

1. Black
2. Blue
3. Light Blue
4. Brown
5. Dark Red
6. Orange
7. Yellow
8. Purple
9. Pink
10. Gold
11. Green
12. Gold
13. Red
14. Dark Green

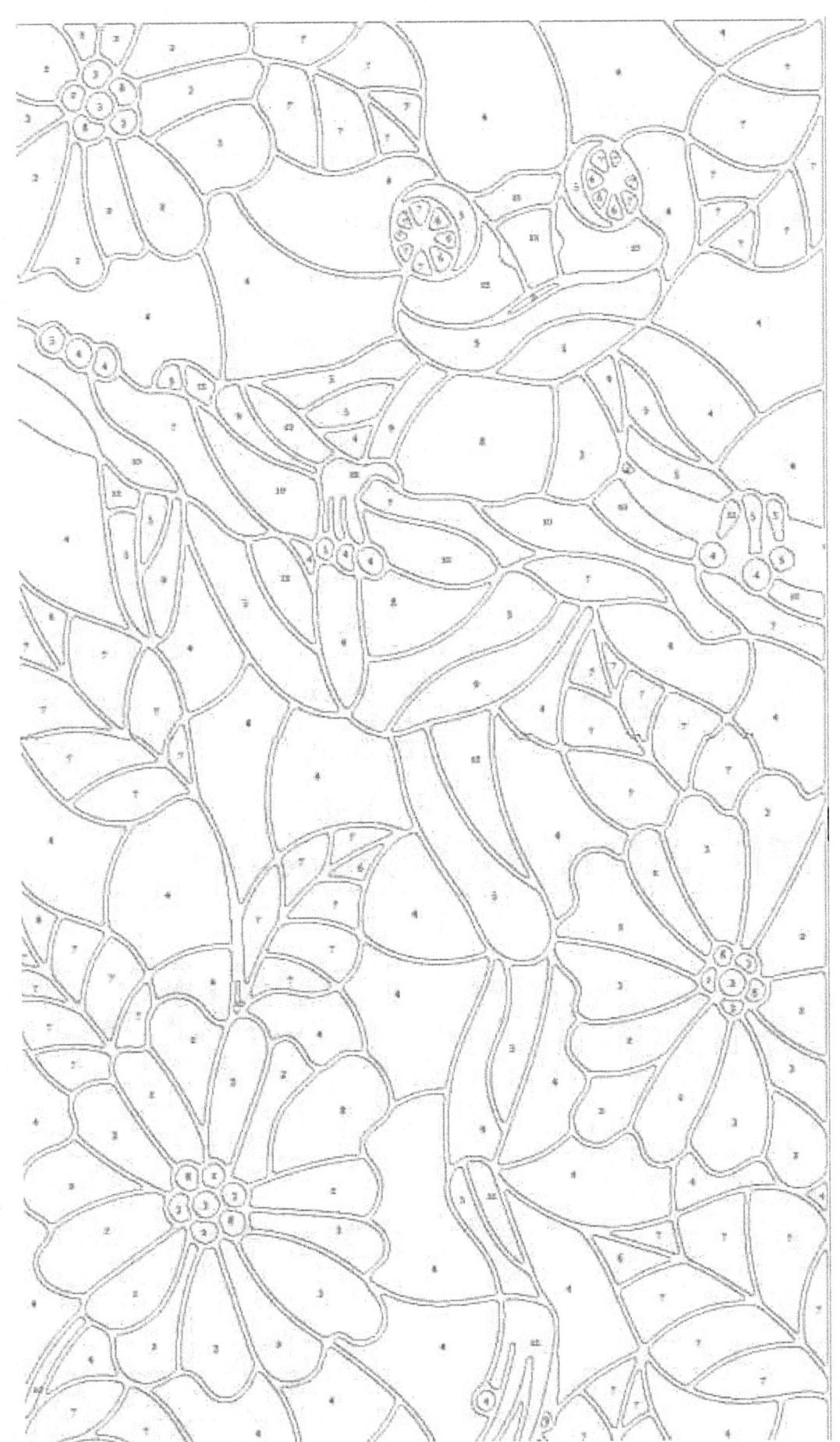

1. Black
2. Blue
3. Light Blue
4. Brown
5. Dark Red
6. Orange
7. Yellow
8. Purple
9. Pink
10. Gold
11. Green
12. Gold
13. Red
14. Dark Green

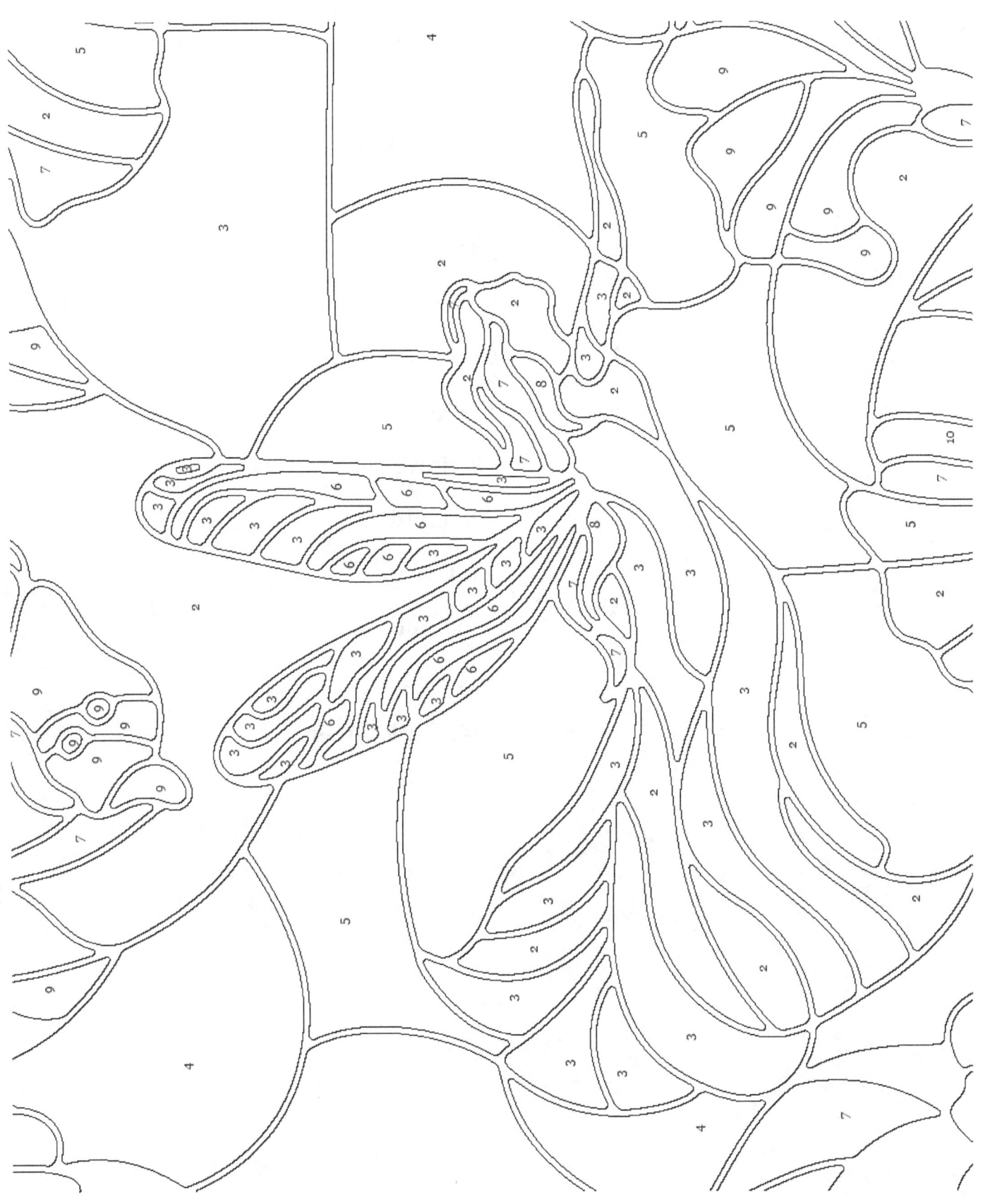

1. Black
2. Blue
3. Light Blue
4. Brown
5. Dark Red
6. Orange
7. Yellow
8. Purple
9. Pink
10. Gold
11. Green
12. Gold
13. Red
14. Dark Green

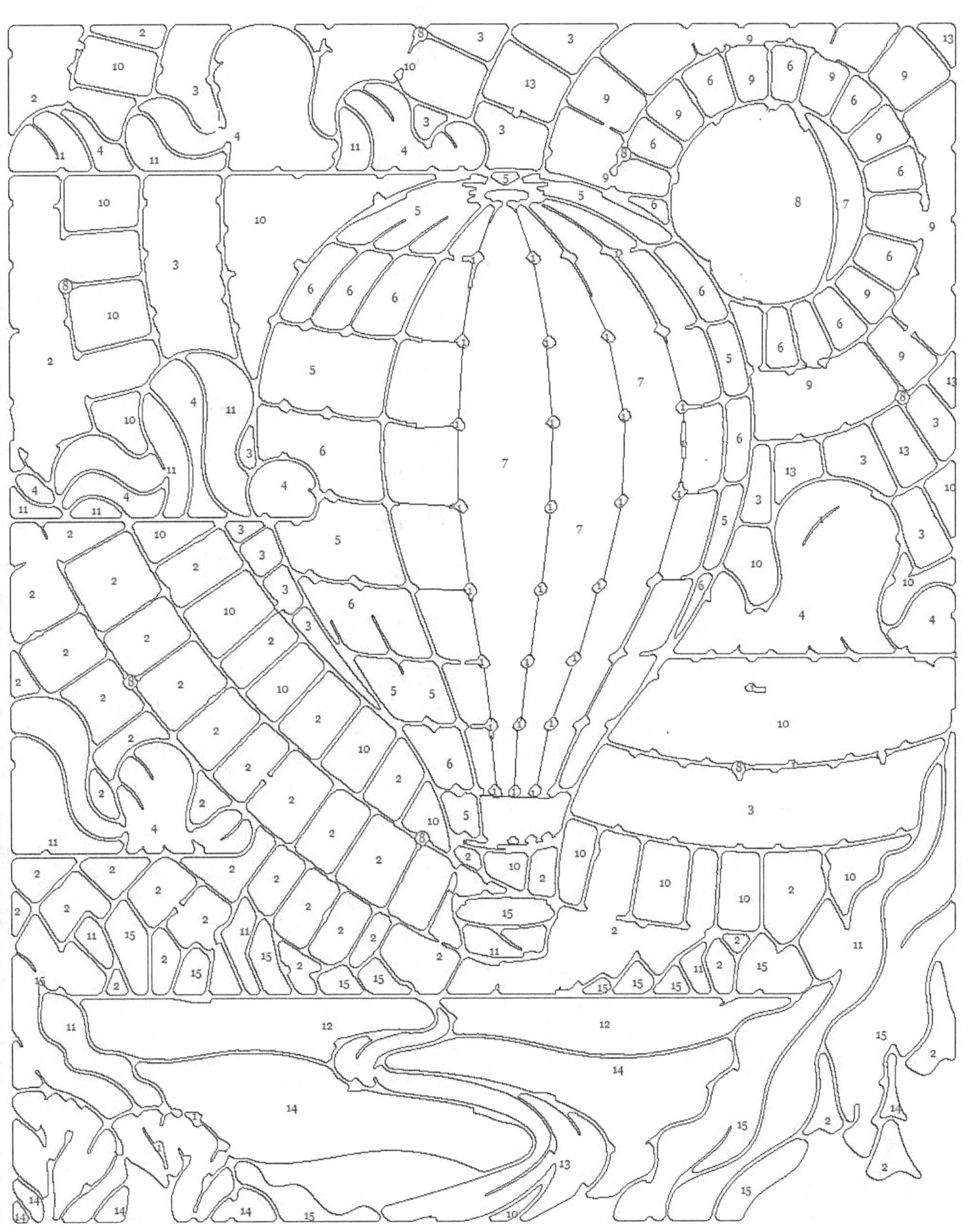

1. Black
2. Blue
3. Light Blue
4. Brown
5. Dark Red
6. Orange
7. Yellow
8. Purple
9. Pink
10. Gold
11. Green
12. Gold
13. Red
14. Dark Green

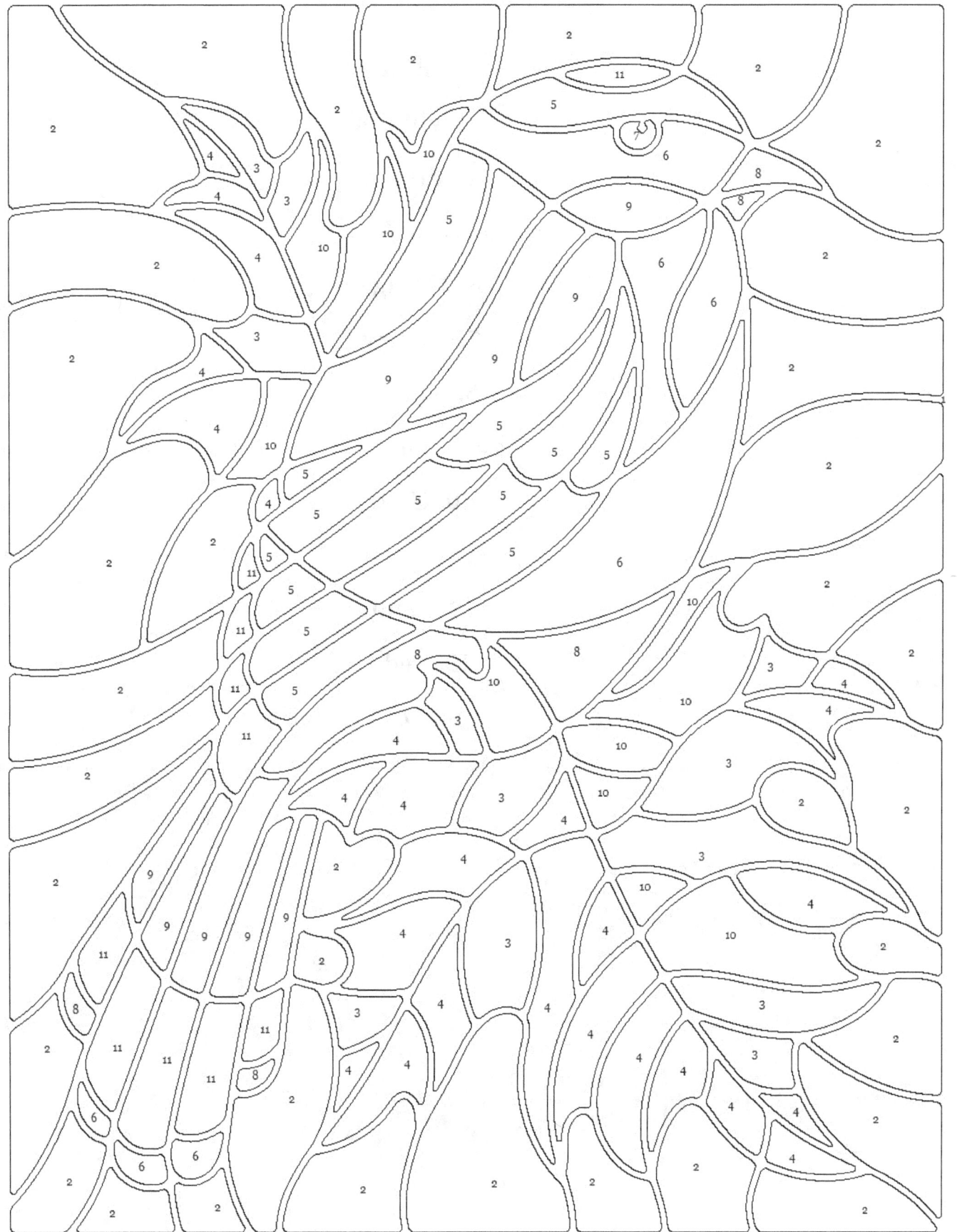

1. Black
2. Blue
3. Light Blue
4. Brown
5. Dark Red
6. Orange
7. Yellow
8. Purple
9. Pink
10. Gold
11. Green
12. Gold
13. Red
14. Dark Green

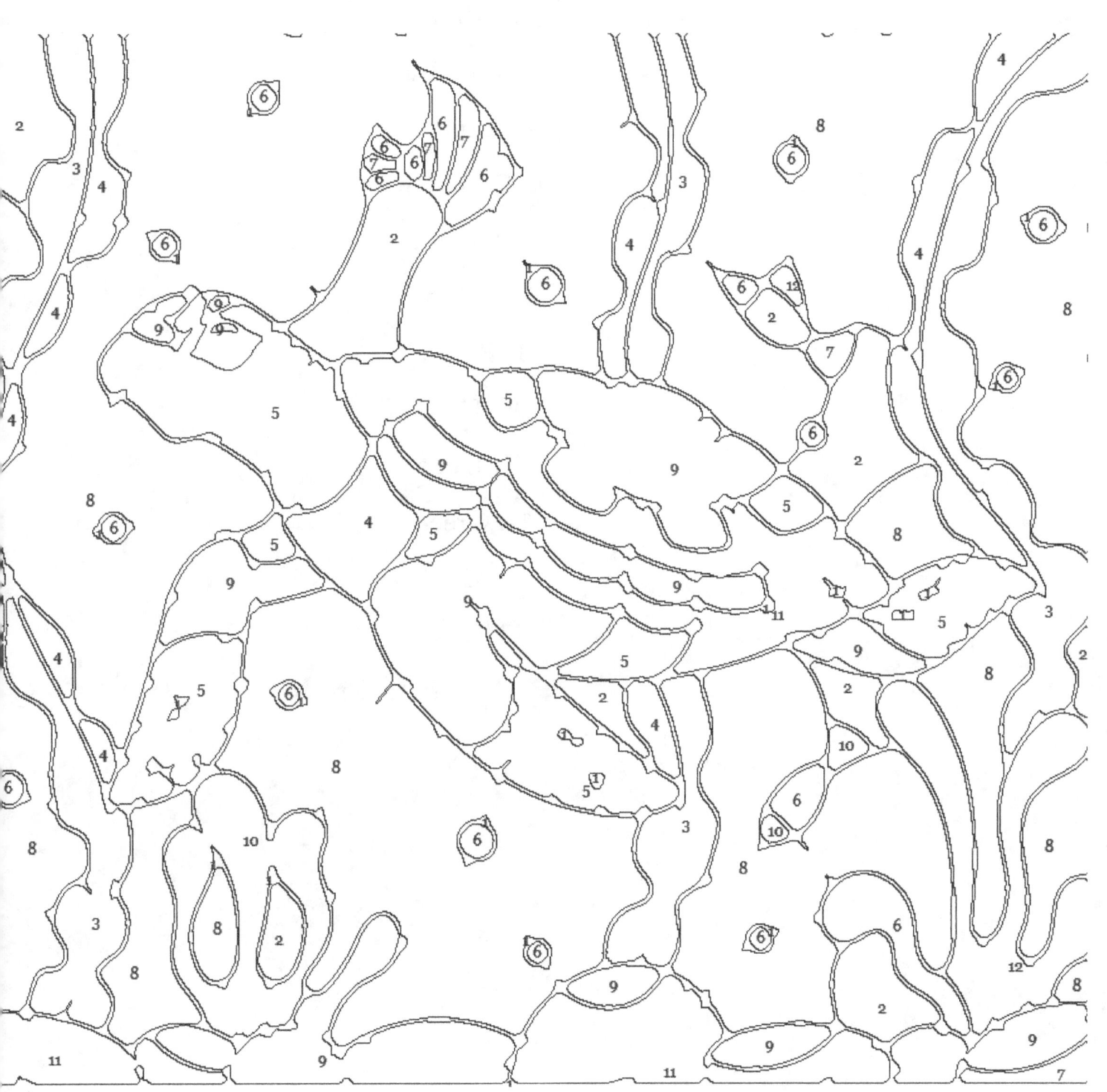

1. Black
2. Blue
3. Light Blue
4. Brown
5. Dark Red
6. Orange
7. Yellow
8. Purple
9. Pink
10. Gold
11. Green
12. Gold
13. Red
14. Dark Green

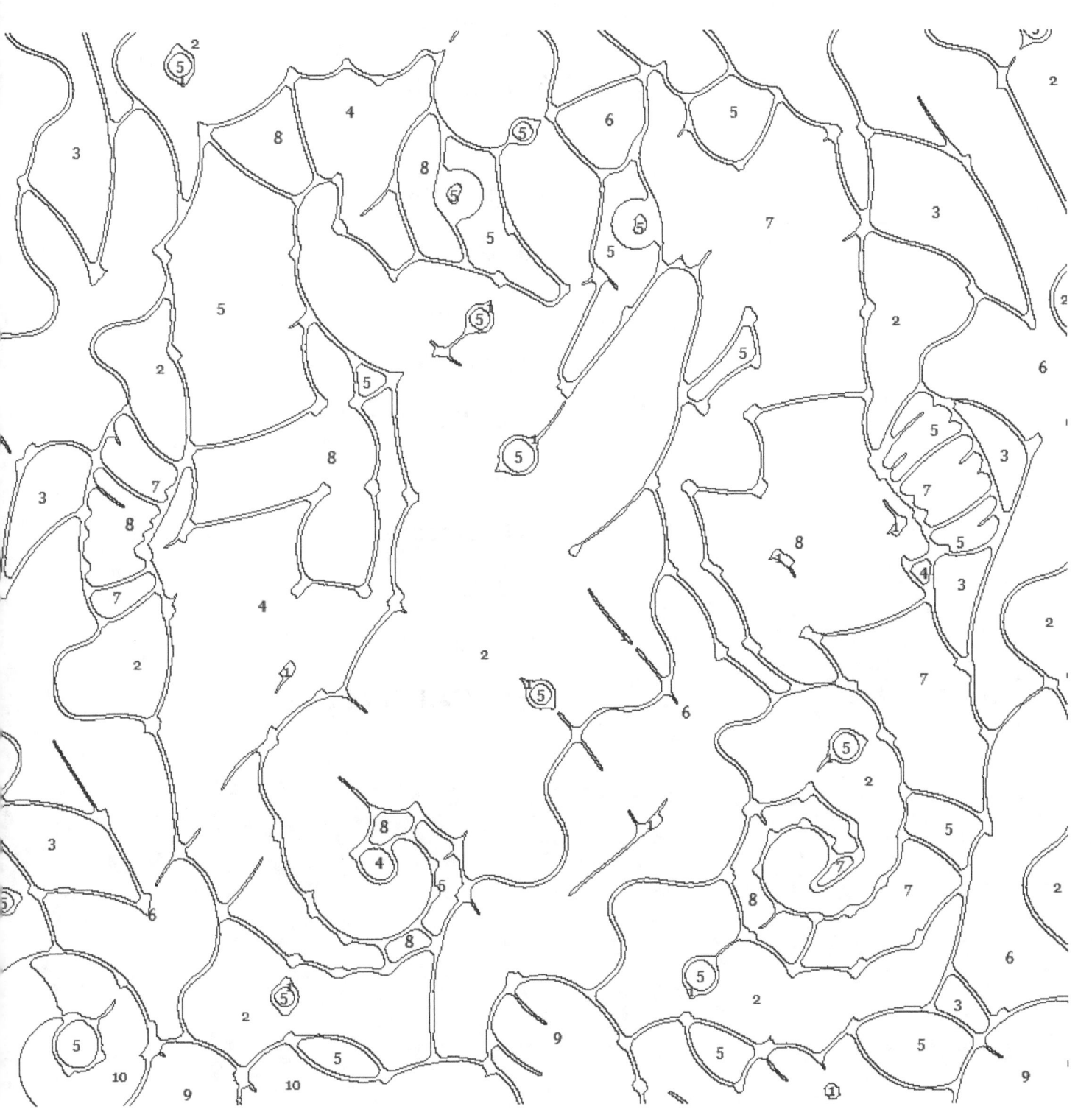

1. Black
2. Blue
3. Light Blue
4. Brown
5. Dark Red
6. Orange
7. Yellow
8. Purple
9. Pink
10. Gold
11. Green
12. Gold
13. Red
14. Dark Green

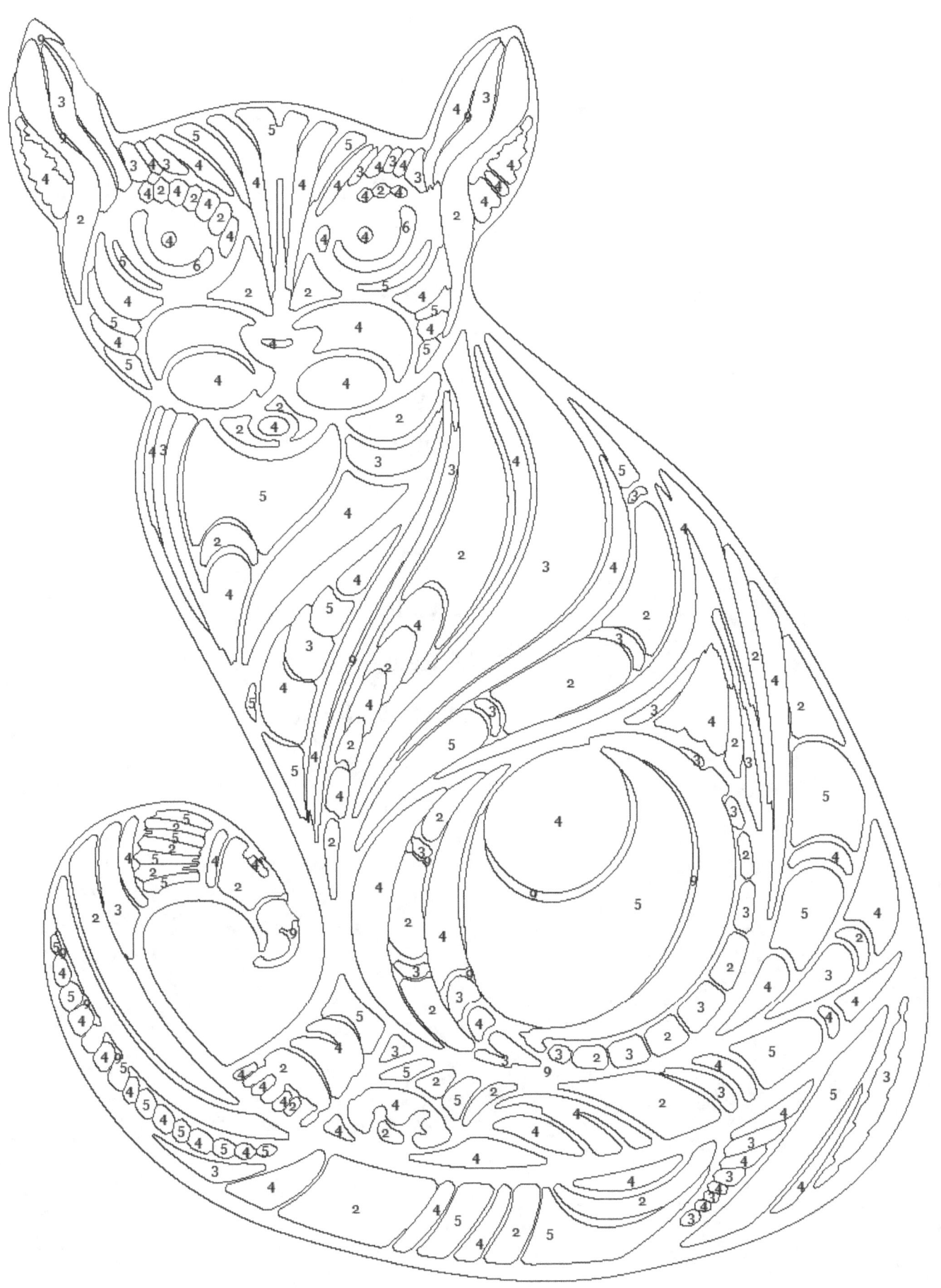

1. Black
2. Blue
3. Light Blue
4. Brown
5. Dark Red
6. Orange
7. Yellow
8. Purple
9. Pink
10. Gold
11. Green
12. Gold
13. Red
14. Dark Green

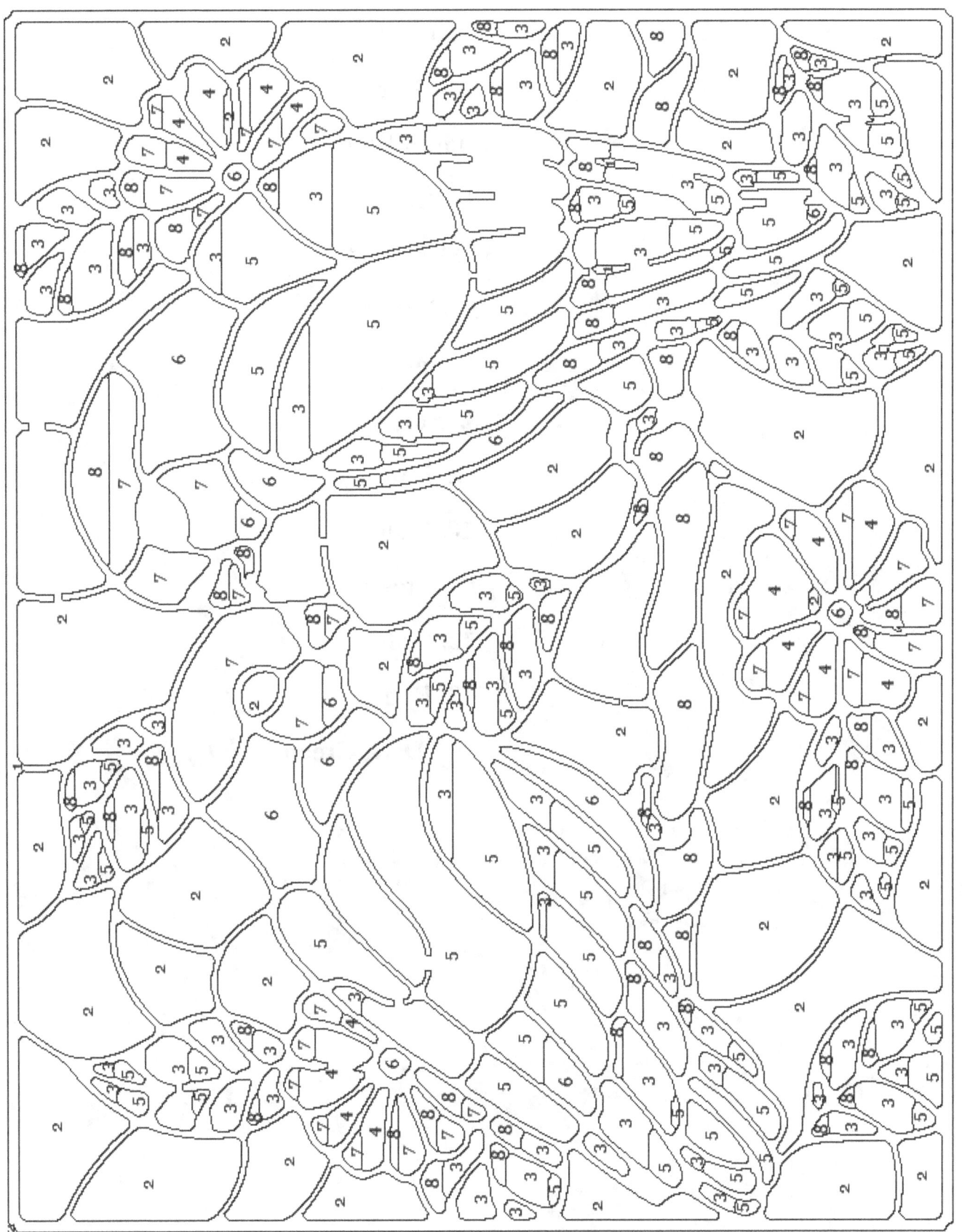

1. Black
2. Blue
3. Light Blue
4. Brown
5. Dark Red
6. Orange
7. Yellow
8. Purple
9. Pink
10. Gold
11. Green
12. Gold
13. Red
14. Dark Green

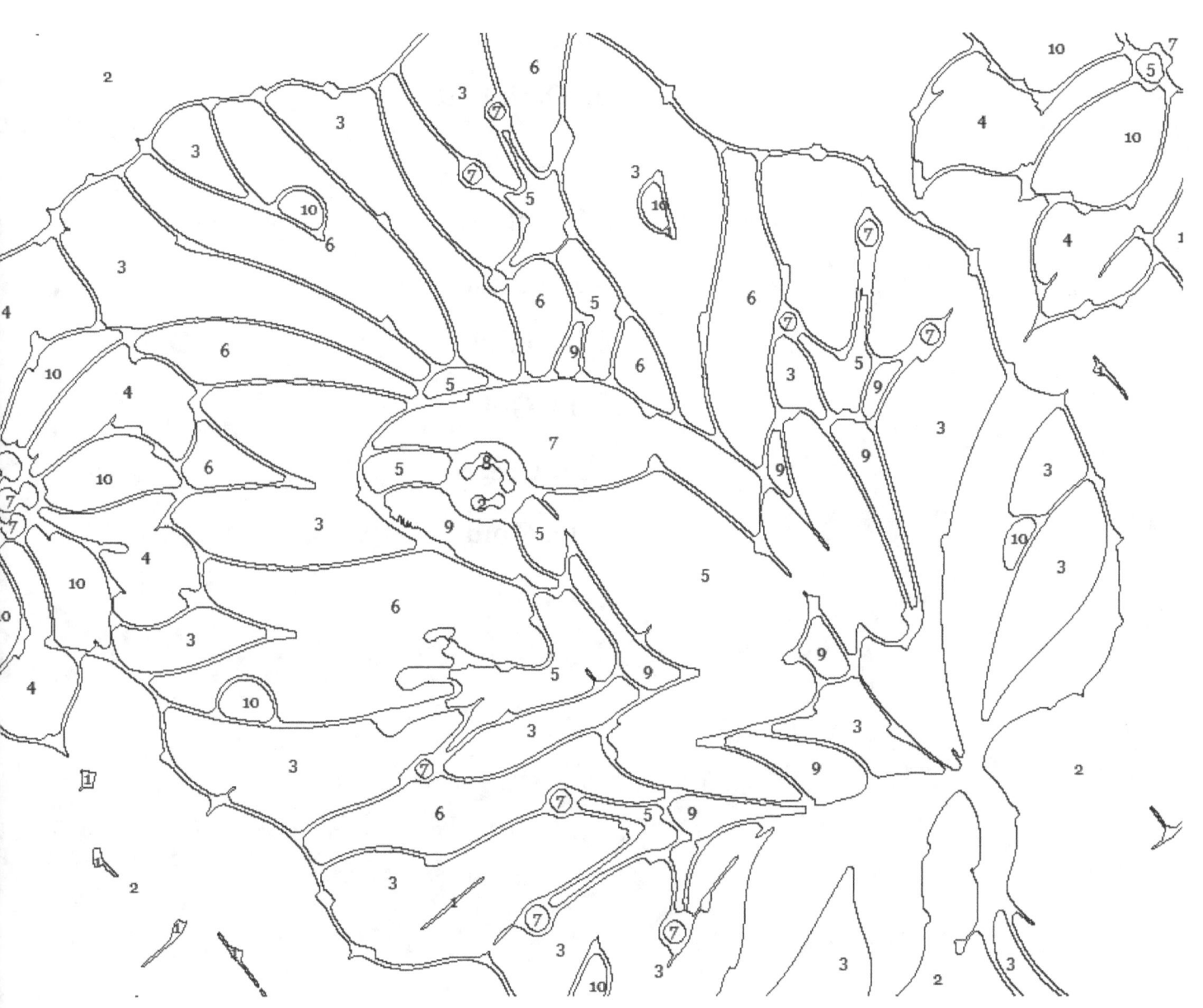

1. Black
2. Blue
3. Light Blue
4. Brown
5. Dark Red
6. Orange
7. Yellow
8. Purple
9. Pink
10. Gold
11. Green
12. Gold
13. Red
14. Dark Green

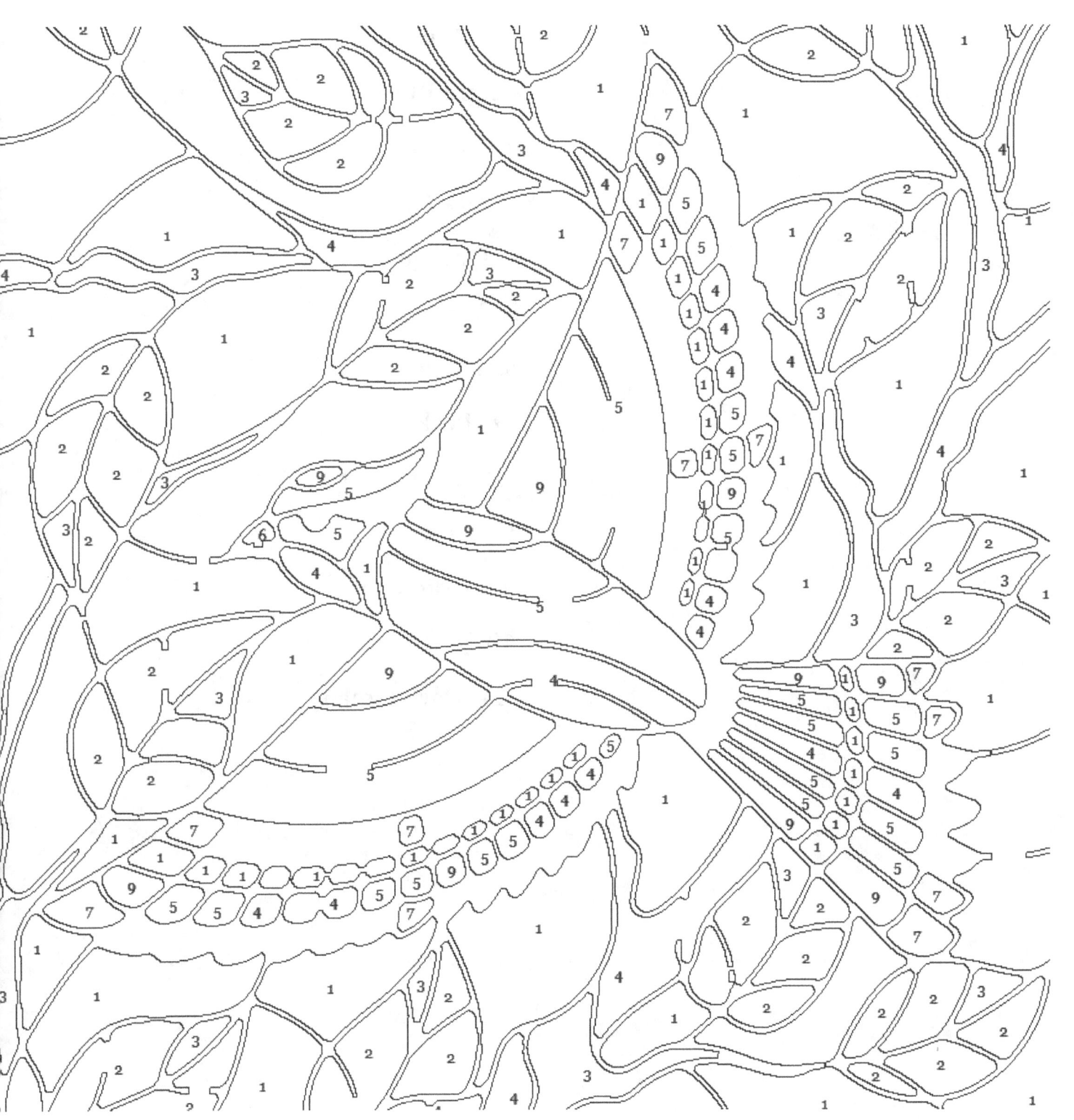

1. Black
2. Blue
3. Light Blue
4. Brown
5. Dark Red
6. Orange
7. Yellow
8. Purple
9. Pink
10. Gold
11. Green
12. Gold
13. Red
14. Dark Green

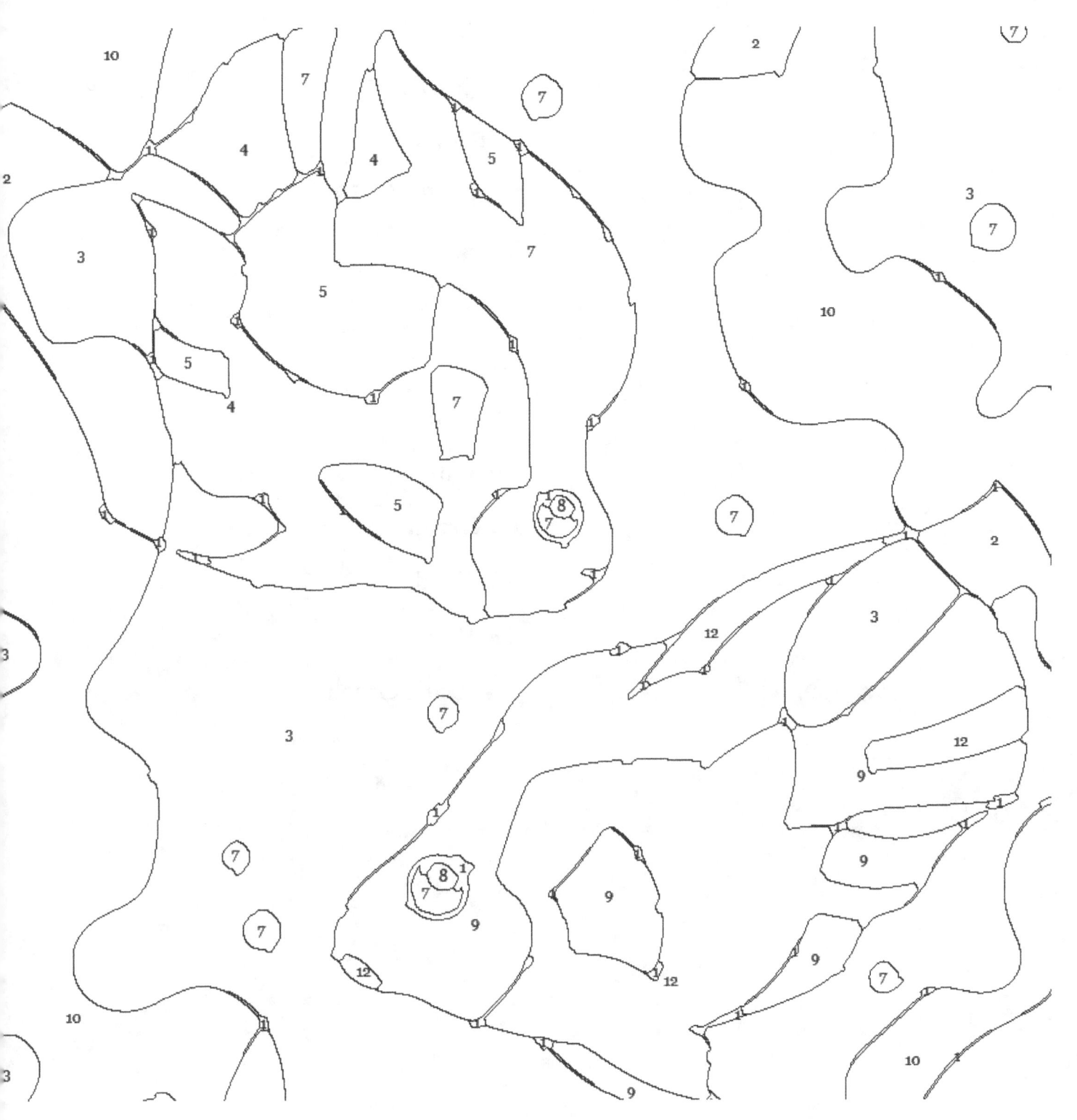

1. Black
2. Blue
3. Light Blue
4. Brown
5. Dark Red
6. Orange
7. Yellow
8. Purple
9. Pink
10. Gold
11. Green
12. Gold
13. Red
14. Dark Green

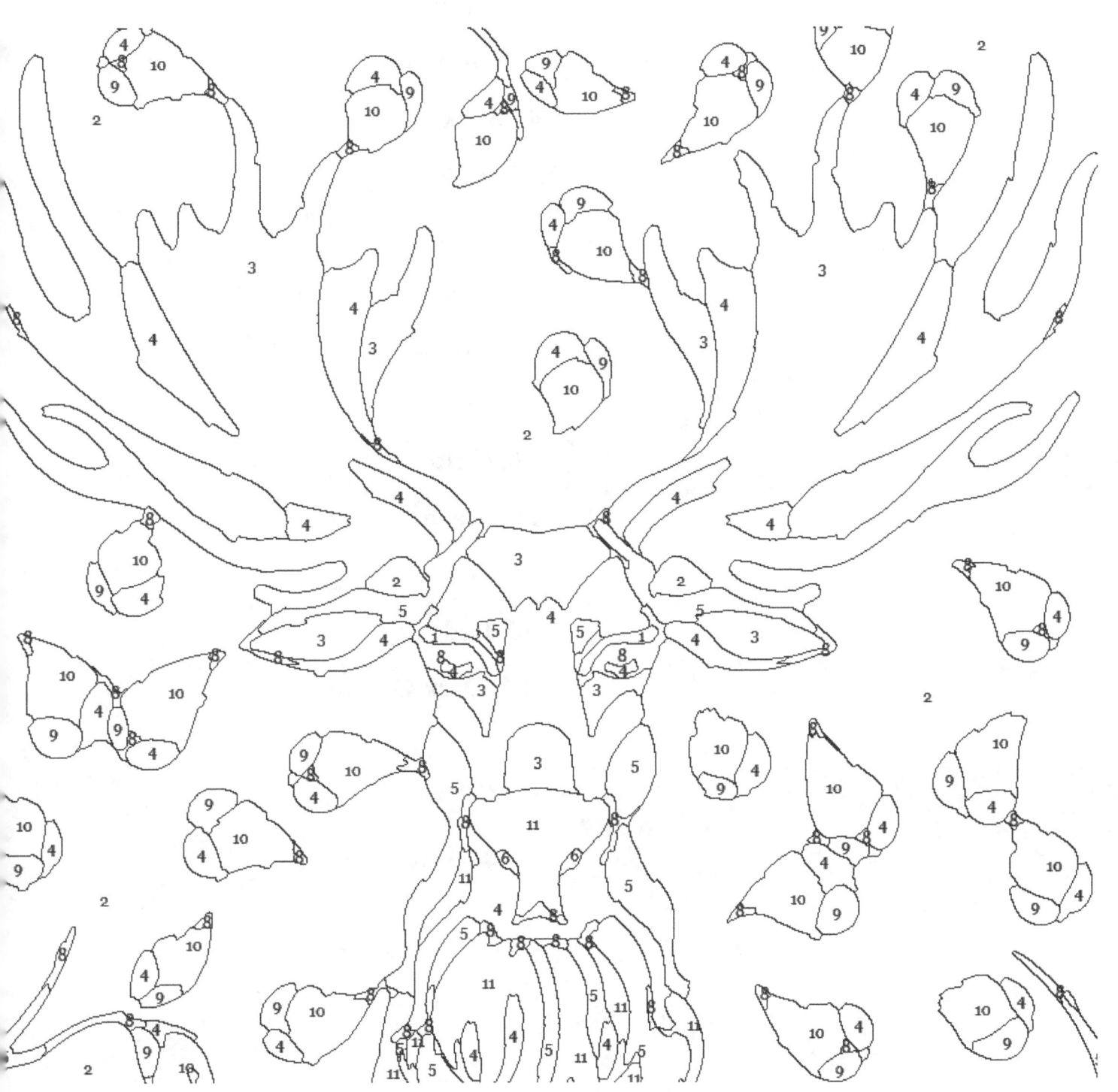

1. Black
2. Blue
3. Light Blue
4. Brown
5. Dark Red
6. Orange
7. Yellow
8. Purple
9. Pink
10. Gold
11. Green
12. Gold
13. Red
14. Dark Green

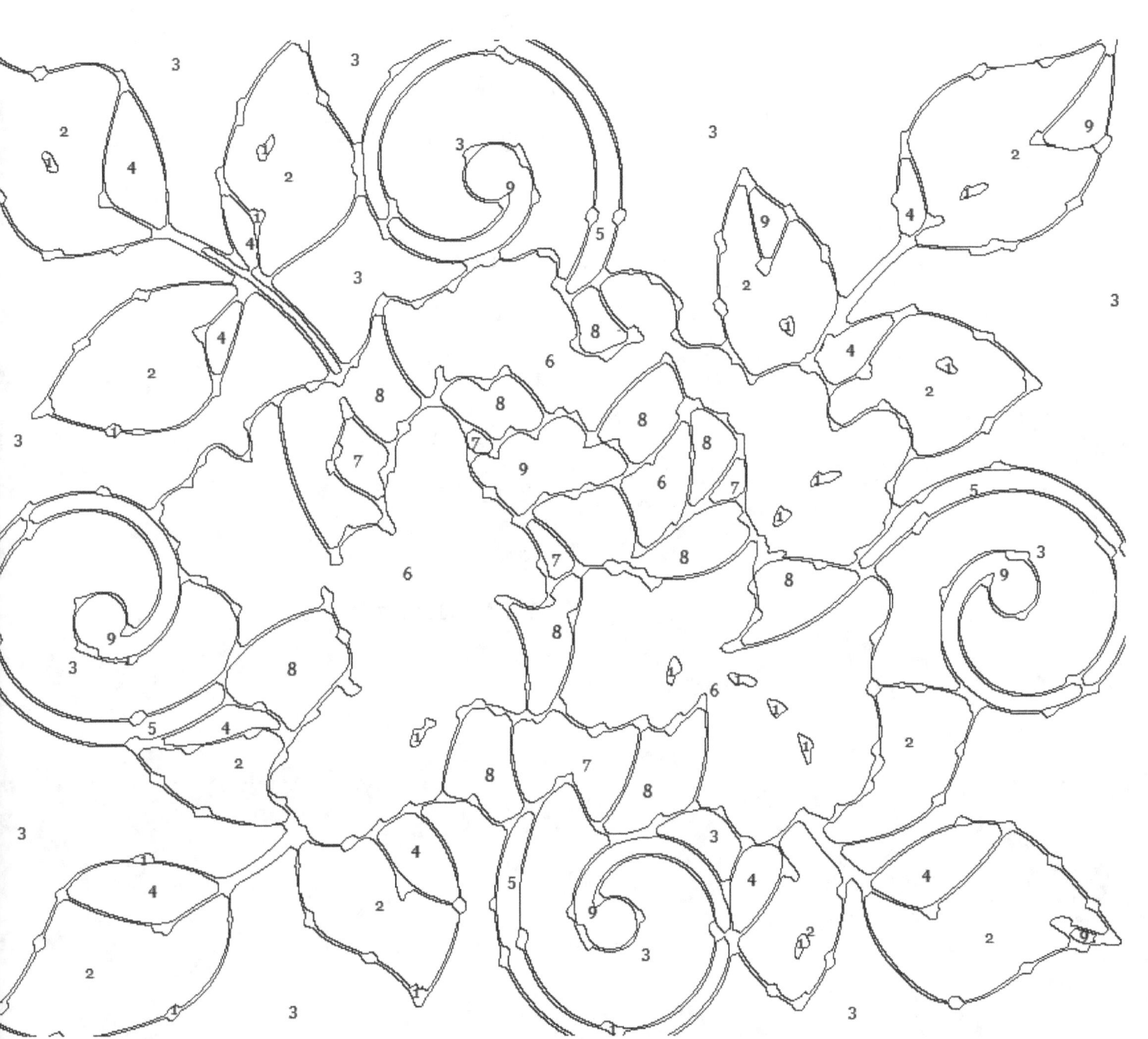

1. Black
2. Blue
3. Light Blue
4. Brown
5. Dark Red
6. Orange
7. Yellow
8. Purple
9. Pink
10. Gold
11. Green
12. Gold
13. Red
14. Dark Green

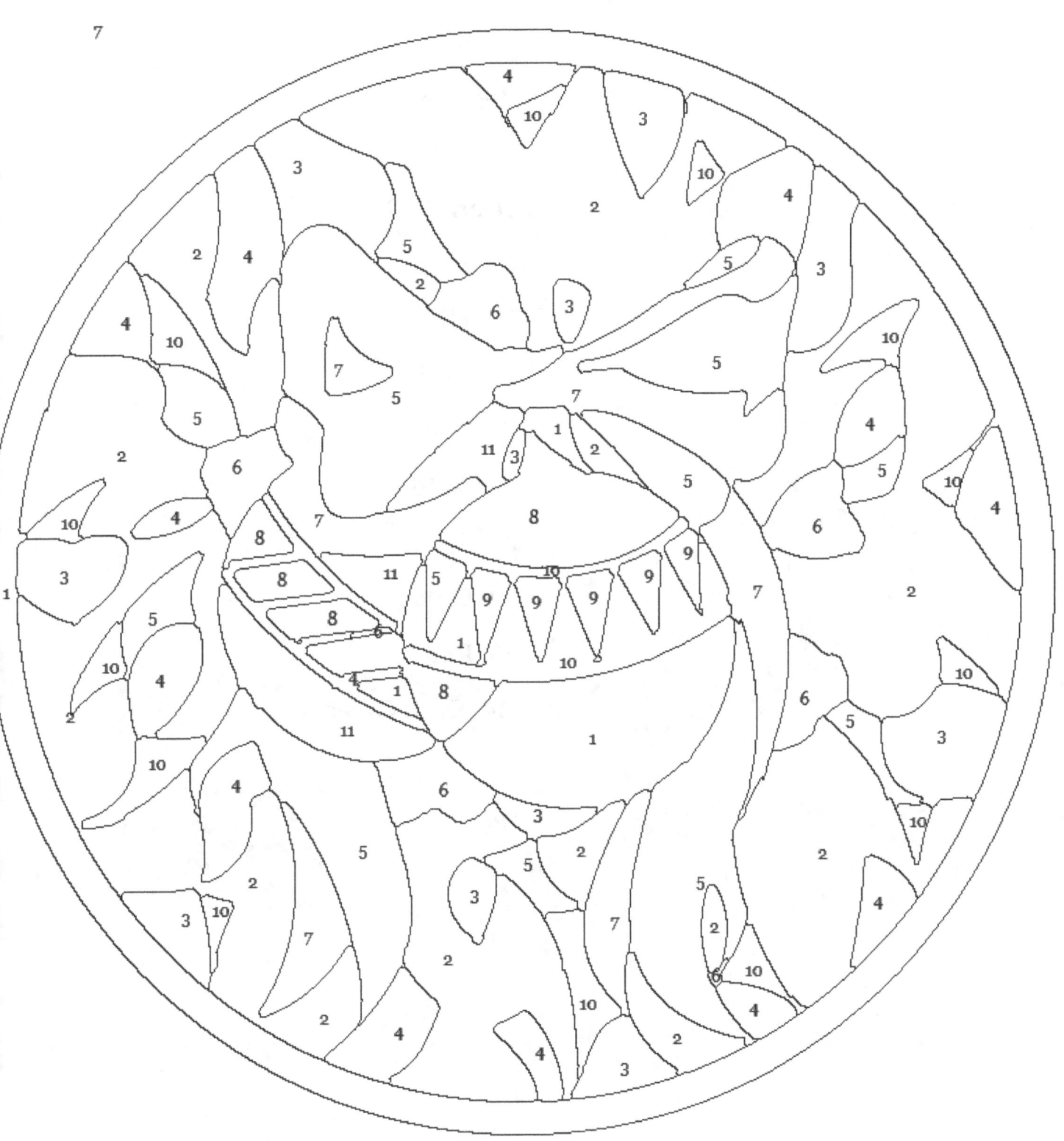

1. Black
2. Blue
3. Light Blue
4. Brown
5. Dark Red
6. Orange
7. Yellow
8. Purple
9. Pink
10. Gold
11. Green
12. Gold
13. Red
14. Dark Green

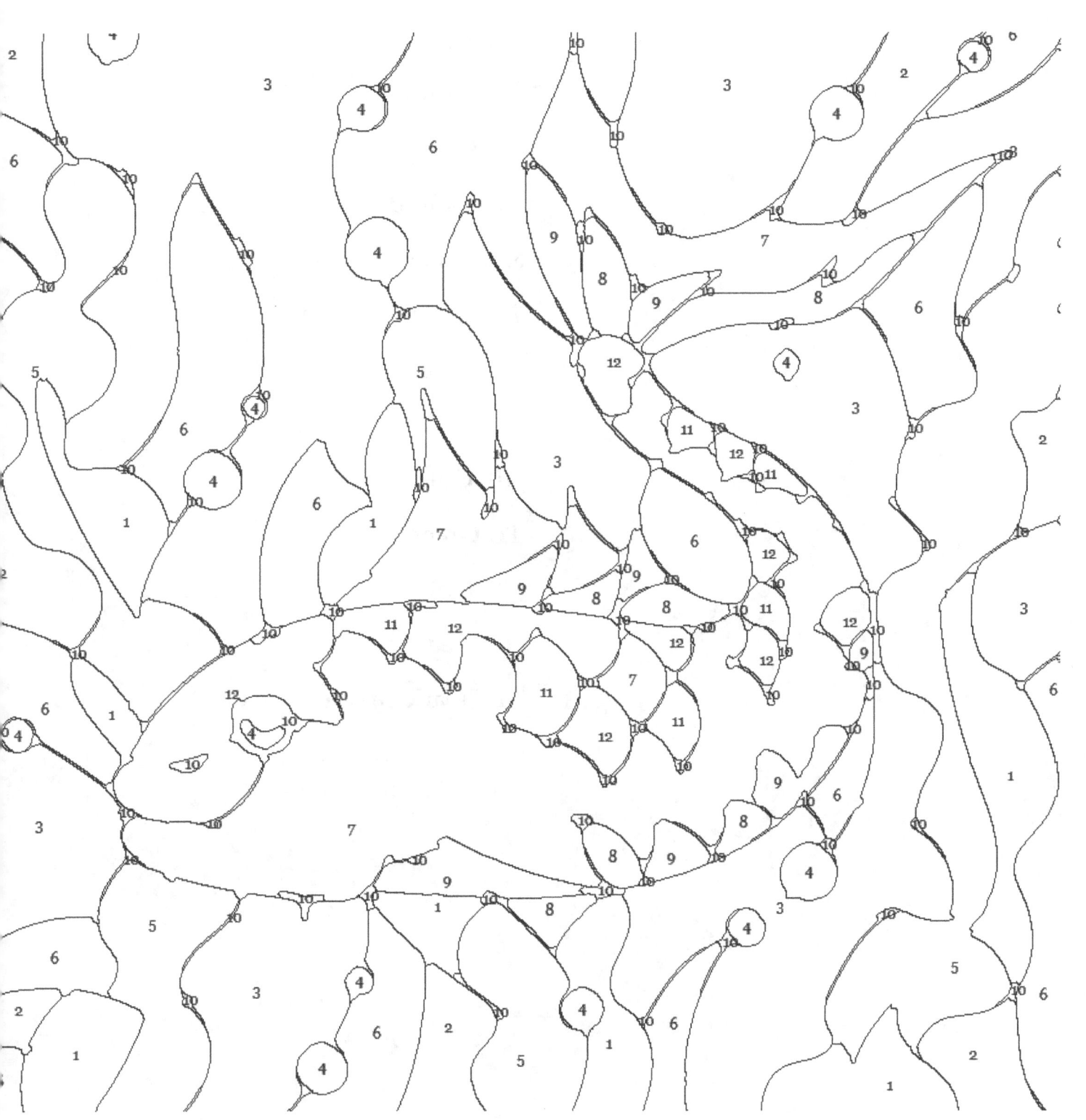

1. Black
2. Blue
3. Light Blue
4. Brown
5. Dark Red
6. Orange
7. Yellow
8. Purple
9. Pink
10. Gold
11. Green
12. Gold
13. Red
14. Dark Green

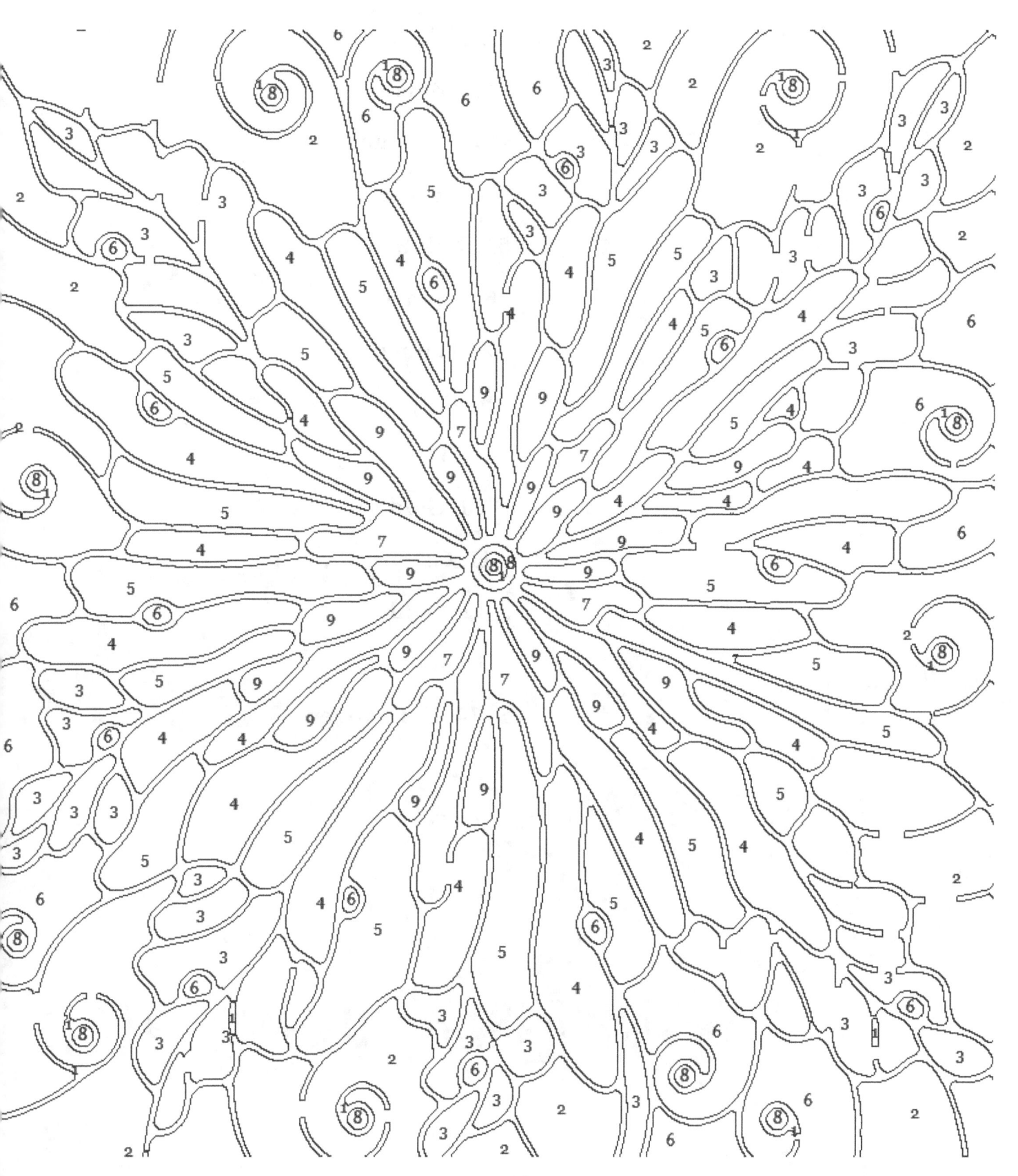

1. Black
2. Blue
3. Light Blue
4. Brown
5. Dark Red
6. Orange
7. Yellow
8. Purple
9. Pink
10. Gold
11. Green
12. Gold
13. Red
14. Dark Green

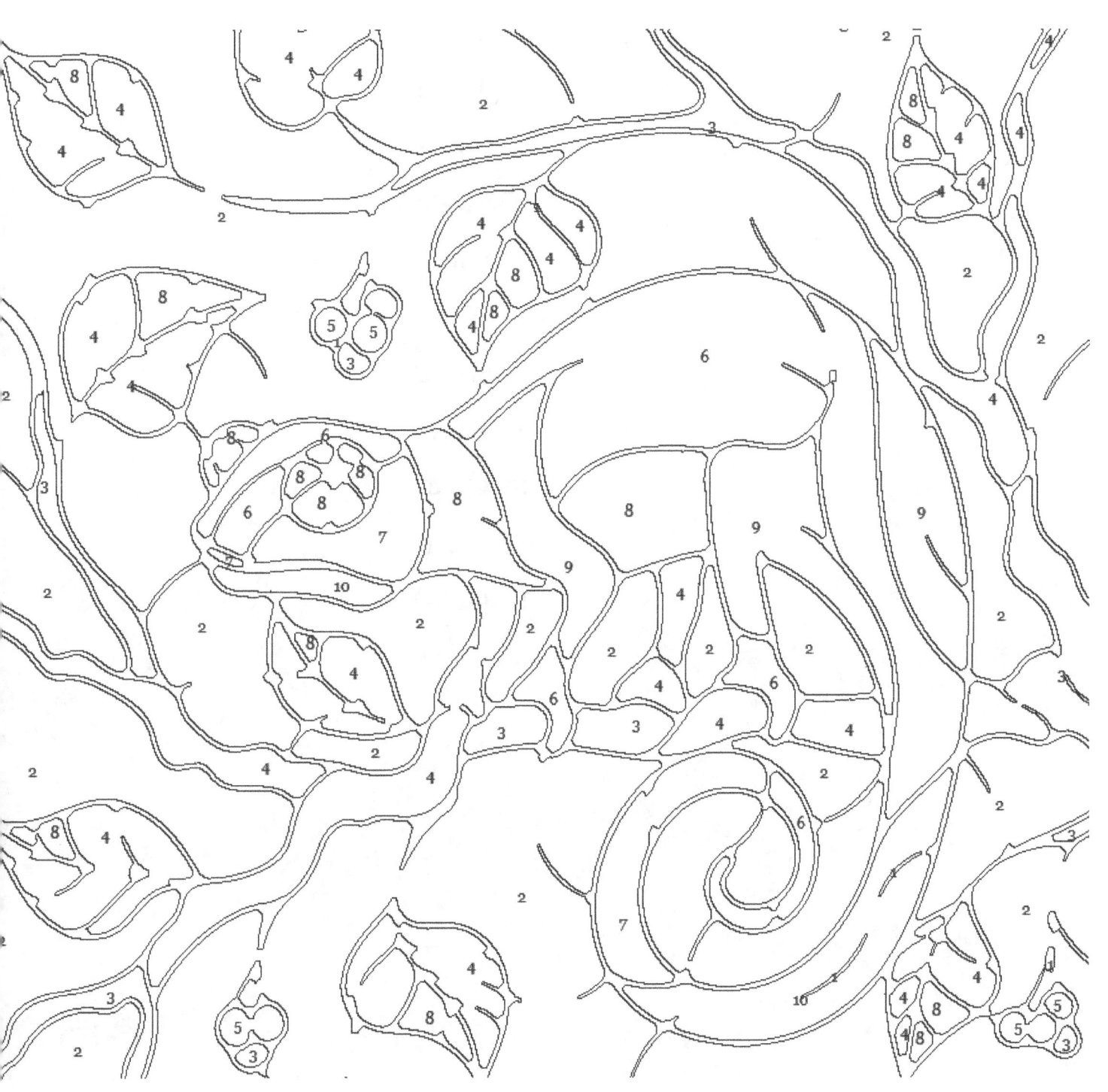

1. Black
2. Blue
3. Light Blue
4. Brown
5. Dark Red
6. Orange
7. Yellow
8. Purple
9. Pink
10. Gold
11. Green
12. Gold
13. Red
14. Dark Green

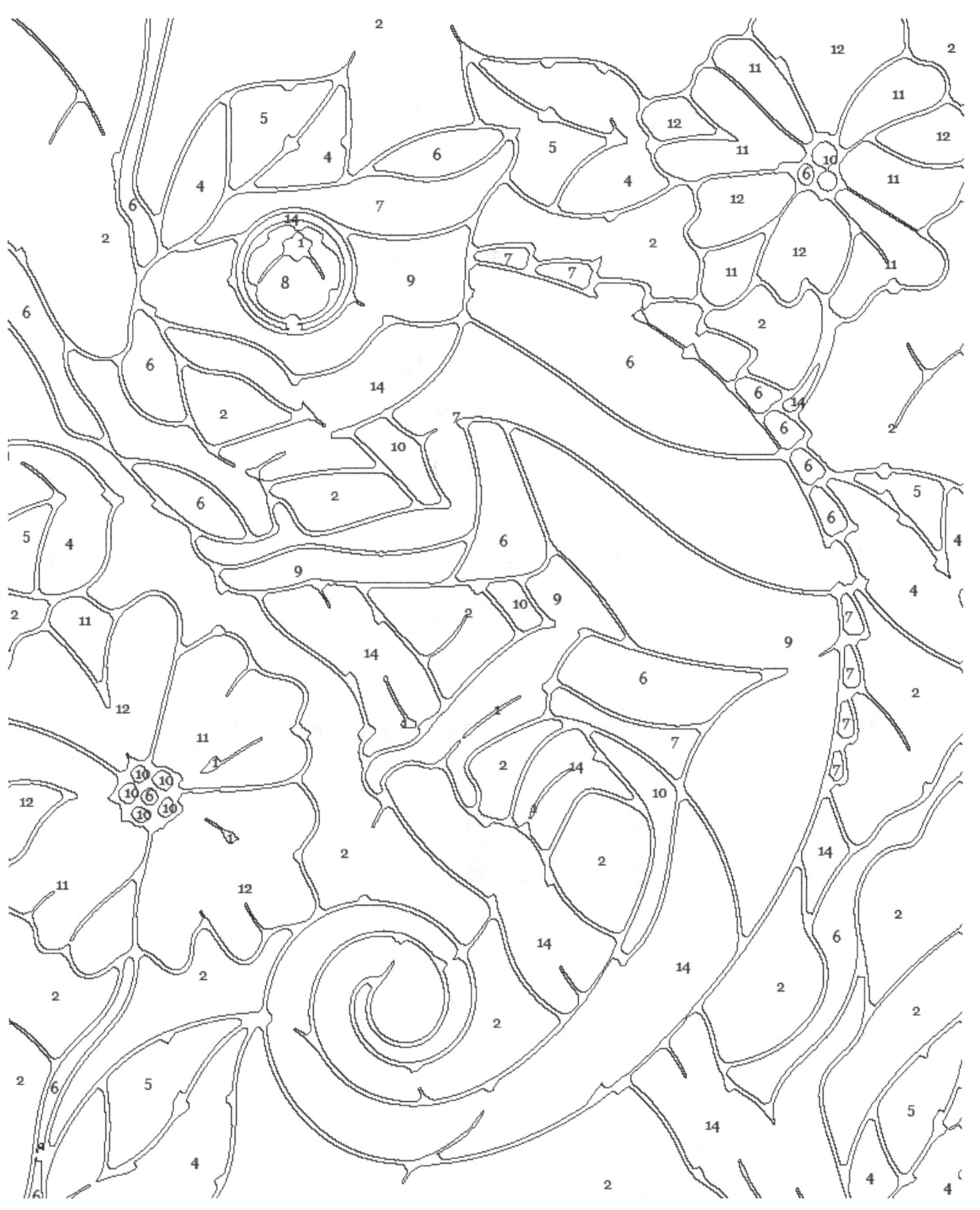

1. Black
2. Blue
3. Light Blue
4. Brown
5. Dark Red
6. Orange
7. Yellow
8. Purple
9. Pink
10. Gold
11. Green
12. Gold
13. Red
14. Dark Green

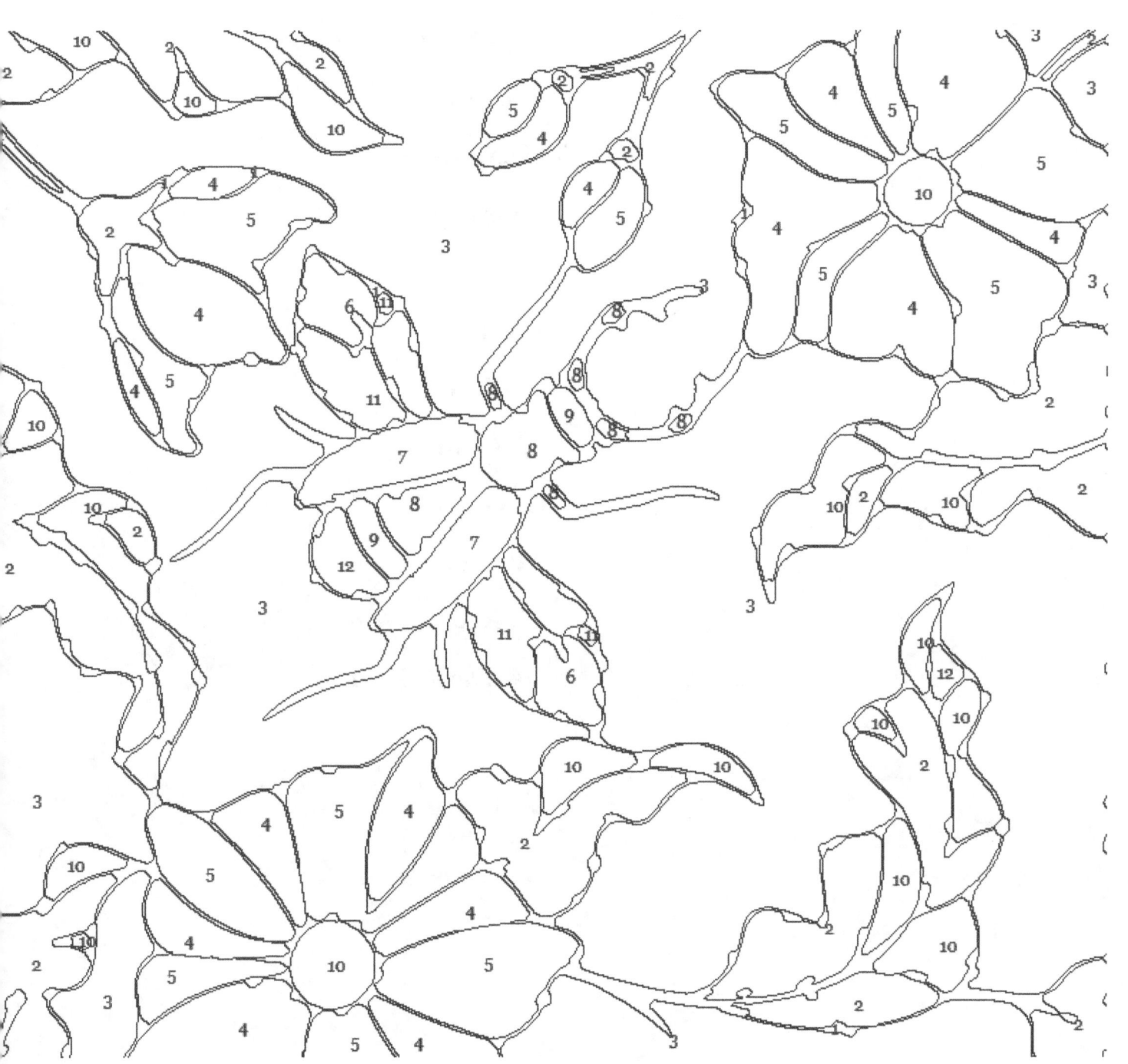

1. Black
2. Blue
3. Light Blue
4. Brown
5. Dark Red
6. Orange
7. Yellow
8. Purple
9. Pink
10. Gold
11. Green
12. Gold
13. Red
14. Dark Green

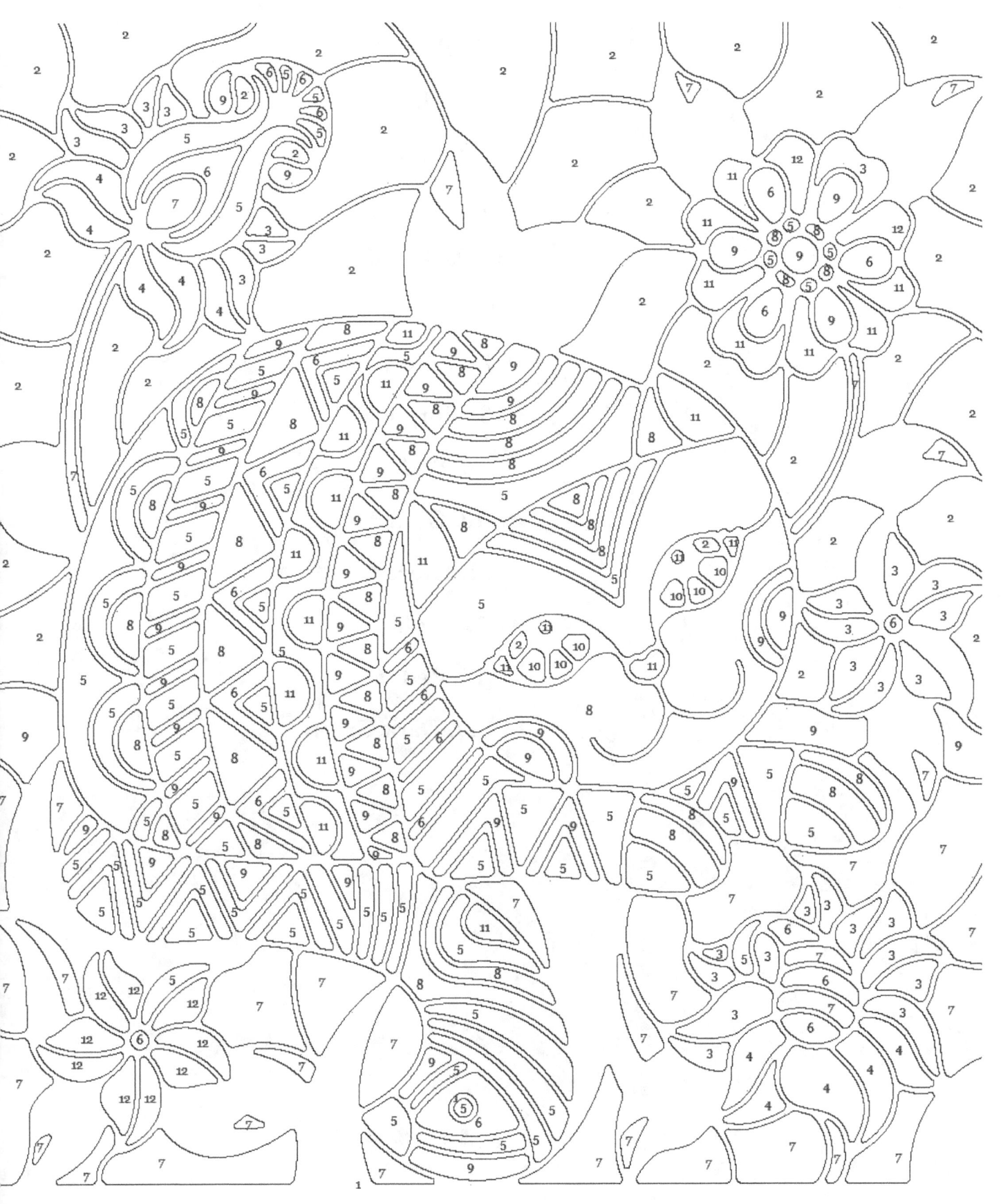

1. Black
2. Blue
3. Light Blue
4. Brown
5. Dark Red
6. Orange
7. Yellow
8. Purple
9. Pink
10. Gold
11. Green
12. Gold
13. Red
14. Dark Green

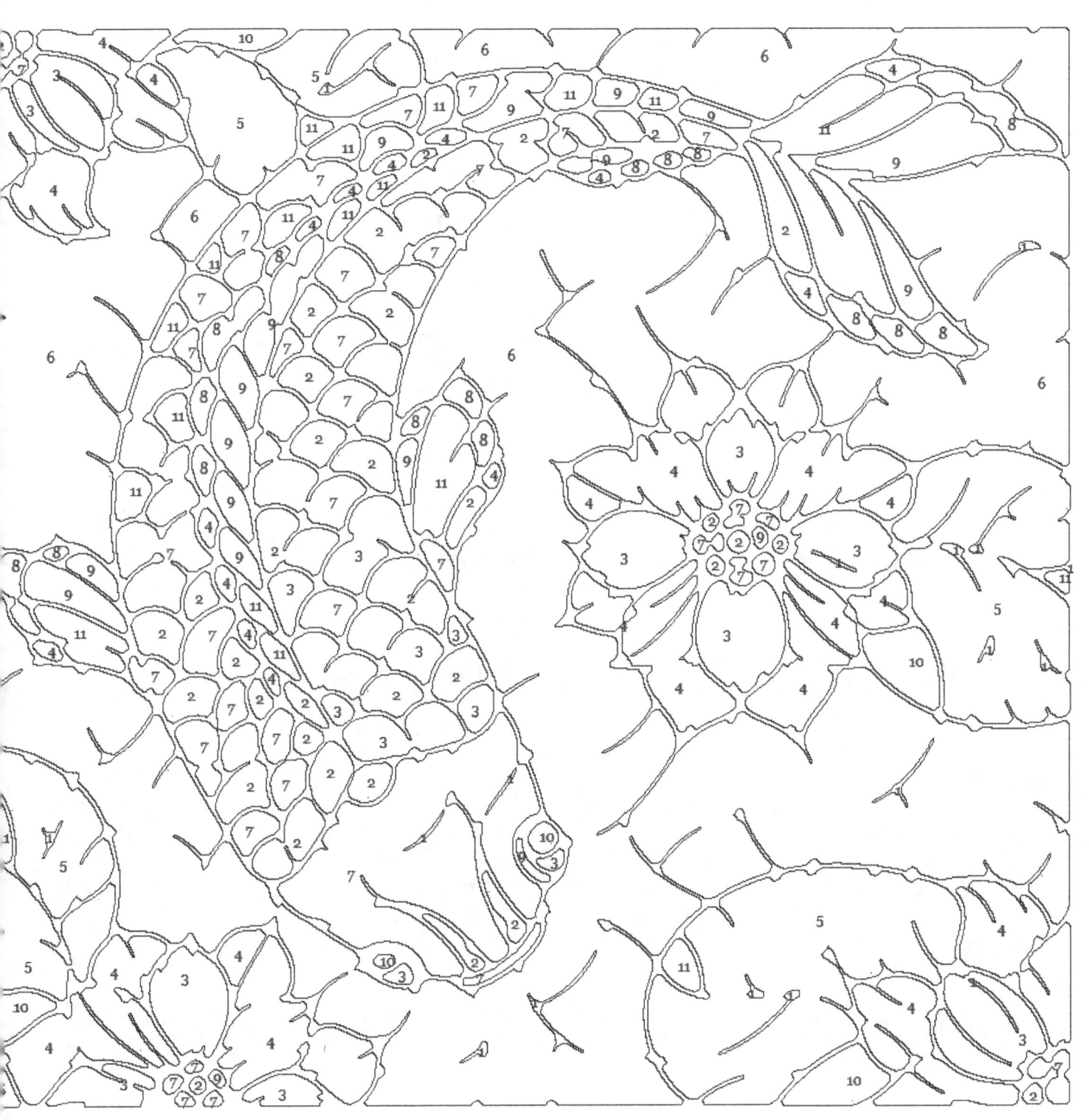

1. Black
2. Blue
3. Light Blue
4. Brown
5. Dark Red
6. Orange
7. Yellow
8. Purple
9. Pink
10. Gold
11. Green
12. Gold
13. Red
14. Dark Green

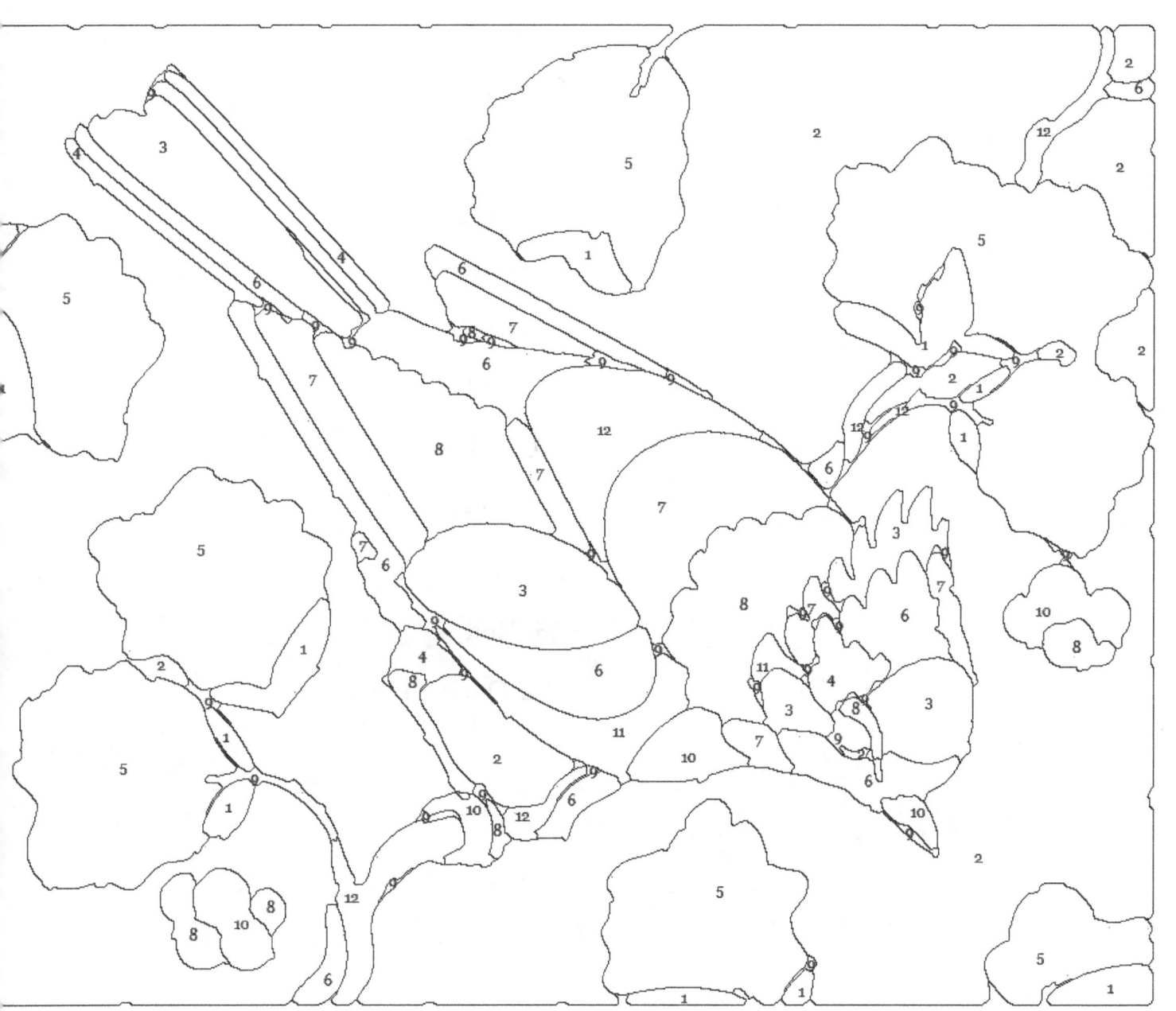

1. Black
2. Blue
3. Light Blue
4. Brown
5. Dark Red
6. Orange
7. Yellow
8. Purple
9. Pink
10. Gold
11. Green
12. Gold
13. Red
14. Dark Green

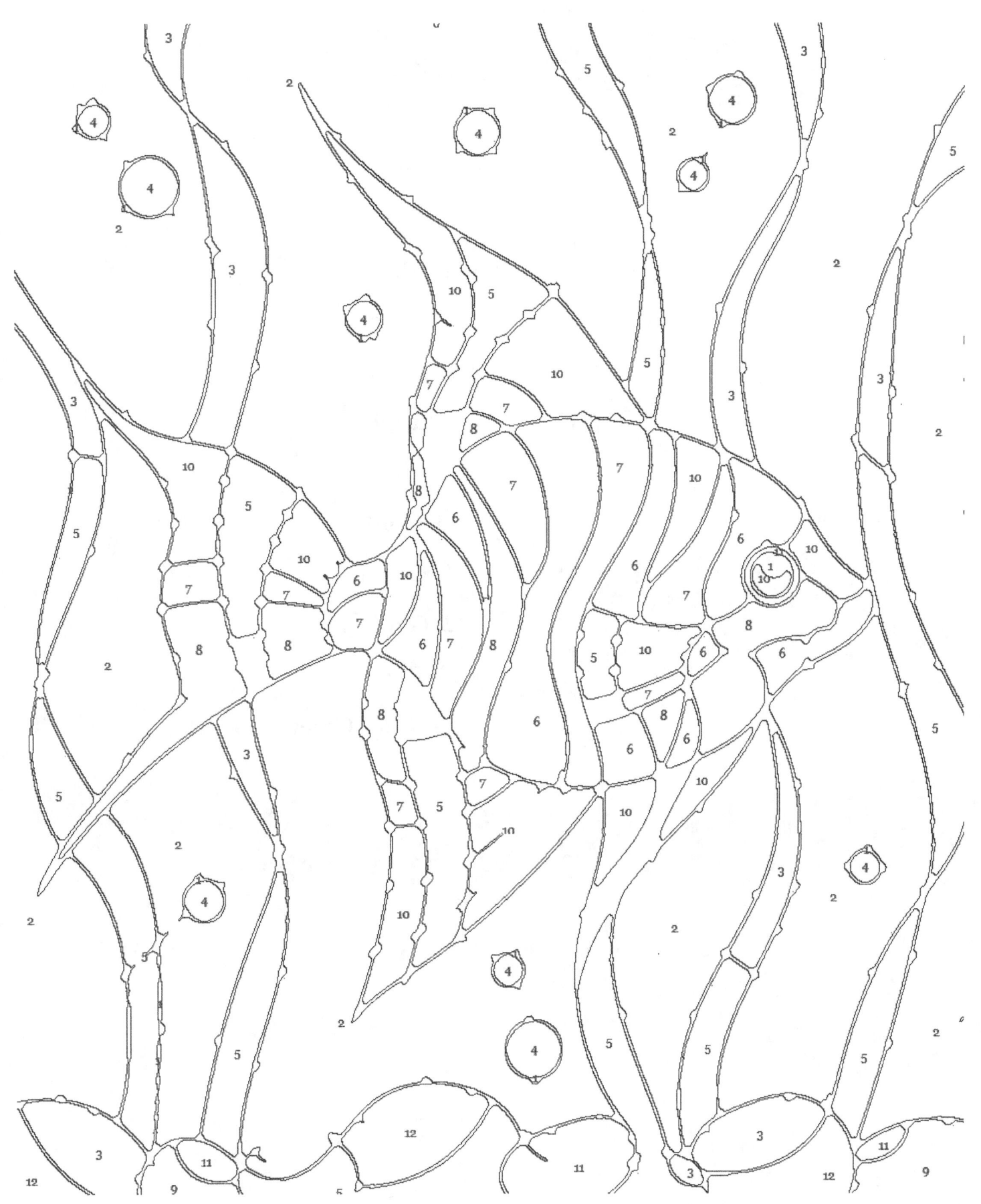

1. Black
2. Blue
3. Light Blue
4. Brown
5. Dark Red
6. Orange
7. Yellow
8. Purple
9. Pink
10. Gold
11. Green
12. Gold
13. Red
14. Dark Green

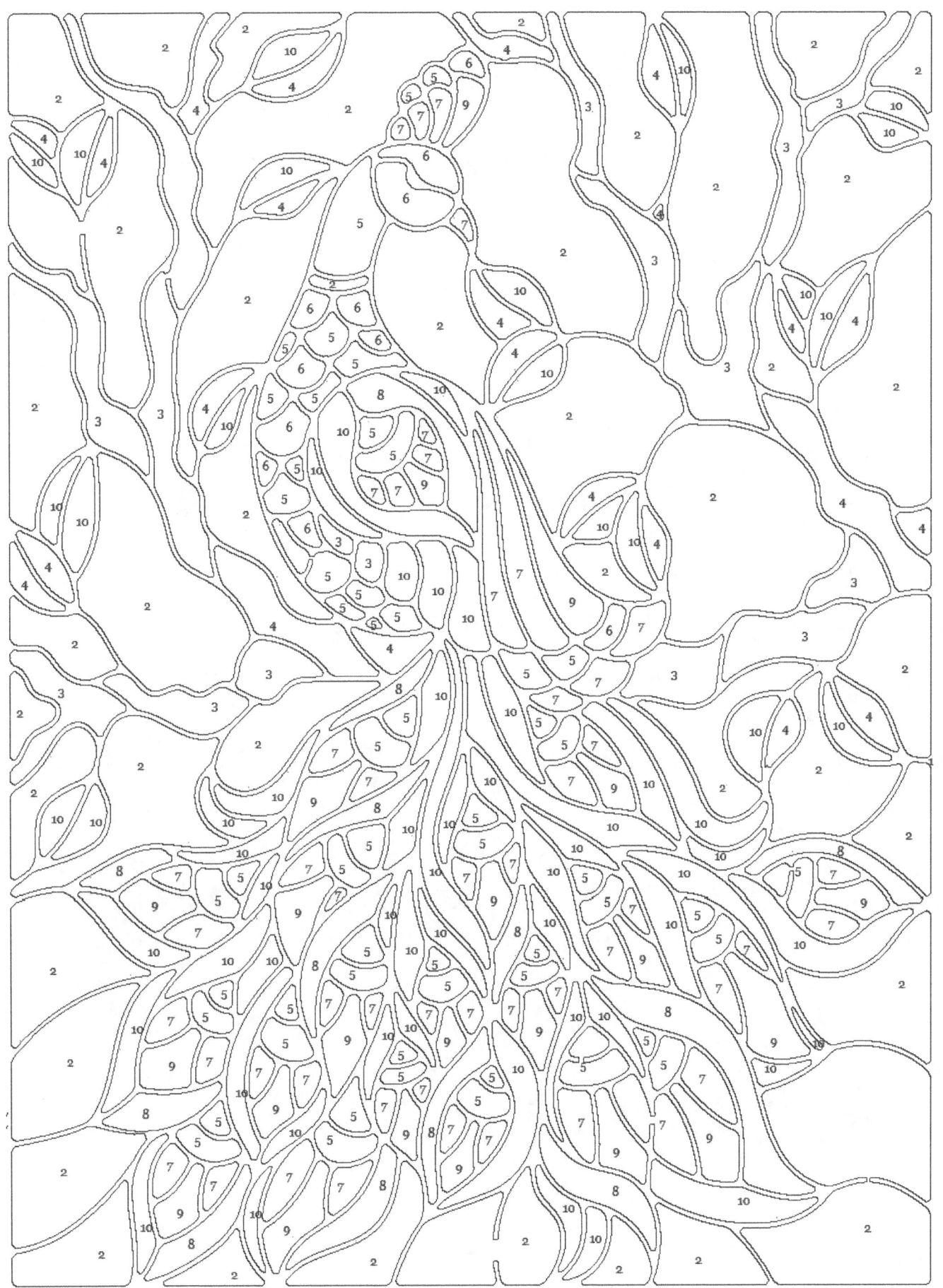